Engage!

How WD-40 Company Built the Engine of Positive Culture

Stan Sewitch

Order this book online at www.trafford.com
or email orders@trafford.com

Most Trafford titles are also available at major online book retailers.

Print information available on the last page.

ISBN: 978-1-6987-1499-8 (sc)
ISBN: 978-1-6987-1501-8 (hc)
ISBN: 978-1-6987-1500-1 (e)

Library of Congress Control Number: 2023913778

Because of the dynamic nature of the Internet, any web addresses or links contained in
this book may have changed since publication and may no longer be valid. The views
expressed in this work are solely those of the author and do not necessarily reflect the
views of the publisher, and the publisher hereby disclaims any responsibility for them.

Any people depicted in stock imagery provided by Getty Images are models, and such
images are being used for illustrative purposes only.
Certain stock imagery © Getty Images.

Trafford rev. 07/28/2023

 www.trafford.com
North America & international
toll-free: 844-688-6899 (USA & Canada)
fax: 812 355 4082

CONTENTS

FOREWORD by Garry Ridge

G'day,

Creating a sustainable, enduring culture of high engagement is not a means to an end. It is the goal, in and of itself.

As a CEO, you know how important culture is to the quality of life that you and everyone else experiences. You also know that culture can have a dramatic impact on results. But you don't work to create a positive culture just so you can grow profits. If that is your motivation, your efforts will fall flat.

In the 25 years that I served as CEO of WD-40 Company, and truly for my entire 35-year career with the company, I was on a journey of learning. When I first accepted the role of CEO in 1997, I was consciously incompetent. I was acutely aware of my status as a novice in the job. So, I set about learning how to be the kind of leader that I would want to work for myself.

I went back to school and earned a master's degree in Executive Leadership from the University of San Diego, a program that was focused on the human aspects of leadership, along with the customary business topics. I met Ken Blanchard who, along with others from his organization, comprised key faculty for the program. Ken and others helped me understand what it would take to not only evolve my own abilities, but also help others grow in their leadership skills.

It's all about the people. That became my mantra. I also believed that leadership was about teaching others how to succeed. Ken and I wrote a book about this philosophy, cited later in this book you're reading.

When I met Stan, perhaps five years into my tenure as CEO, I took some time to get to know him. I found that he and I shared the exact same values of leadership and of business. He became an early coach for me, and he helped me continue my evolution. After more than a decade of working together, making steady progress in our goal to continually build a strong, engaged, positive culture comprised of people who loved working together, achieving great things, I asked Stan to come work with me full time.

We continued our partnership, faced numerous challenges, and had many, many wonderful, positive lasting memories on our journey of doing the right thing for our tribe and all the company's stakeholders.

It wasn't easy by any means. We never achieved perfection and didn't expect to. We did achieve a lot, however, as you will read about later. While I'm proud of what Stan, I, our leaders, and our entire tribe accomplished together, I know that there is more to do. That's a good thing. We have passed the leadership baton to others who are now accountable for continuing the journey.

What you will read here is a deeper look under the hood of exactly what it took for us to reach a sustained engagement level of 93%. The "engine" of culture that Stan talks about is an appropriate metaphor. There are many parts, and they all must work together in harmony to result in a humming motor of human engagement.

Stan and I, along with San Diego State University and Purpose Point, decided we needed to bring CEOs together to talk about this engine, to impart more of the methods and principles that we applied to result in such high engagement. The Culture Forum was the result. Increasing engagement is the single largest opportunity for improving the quality of life in the world of work, while concurrently greatly improving the economic opportunities for everyone involved.

I hope you will study this book carefully. Read it a few times. It is a wealth of information gleaned from decades of experience, provided by someone who's only objective is to help you succeed on your path as a CEO leading a great organization where people are the first priority.

Garry Ridge

FOREWORD by Scott Blanchard

I met Garry Ridge more than 25 years ago, when he enrolled in the Master's in Executive Leadership at University of San Diego. The MSEL program was a joint venture between USD and The Ken Blanchard Companies, the family business I have worked in for 30 years. I had the honor of teaching in the program during the inaugural class.

Garry stood out among his peers in his thirst for learning and his determination to take what he learned and directly apply it to WD-40 Company. Fortunately, Garry agreed to serve on the Board of Directors for Blanchard for many years after his studies were complete. During the time Garry served on our Board of Directors, we benefitted so much from his insights as the CEO of WD-40 Company during a period of strong, consistent growth.

From my point of view, Garry possesses three unique traits that have contributed to his success and, by extension, has contributed to the employees, customers and shareholders of WD-40 Company over these past 30 years. Garry has an insatiable need to learn, an even deeper need to apply what he has learned to his business and perhaps even a deeper need to serve others, making a positive difference in people's lives. The combination of these traits, and countless others, have fueled his long and successful journey as CEO of WD-40 Company.

As such, it is no surprise that Garry and Stan Sewitch developed such a strong partnership. Garry was determined to apply the leadership principles and lessons he learned from my dad and other key thought leaders who believed that the long term, sustainable success of an organization was not impossible—but it was contingent upon building an aligned, engaged, focused and determined culture.

In Stan, Garry found a partner who was not only interested in building a strong culture but was equally determined to create and implement each of the critical components necessary to build a values-based, human-powered and sustainable culture that was aligned with the growth and evolution Garry envisioned. Together, and with the dedication and commitment of leaders throughout the organization, Garry and Stan built an incredible culture at WD-40 Company which has fueled decades of strong and steady growth.

Inside this book, you will find great concepts and principles necessary to build a strong culture. But more importantly, you will learn *how* these principles have been applied over decades, in concert with each other. The culture WD-40 Company achieved was built carefully, one piece at a time: values, purpose and strategy—compensation, performance leadership coaching—human development at all levels—hiring, transparency, belonging and inclusion. Every critical component to building a resilient and lasting culture aligned with growth has been intentionally designed.

I understand the approach that Stan and Garry have developed intimately, because I sought out their help a little more than a year into my tenure as president of Blanchard, which began in January of 2020, just in time for the arrival of a global pandemic. As we navigated the sharp downturn in business that resulted from the virtual lockdown of in-person life and work, we faced an incredible challenge and an equally incredible opportunity to reinvent Blanchard as a company and as a culture. With the full support of our family ownership group and with the partnership of my CHRO Kristin Costello, I sought out Garry's advice on implementing a profit-sharing incentive program, that was aligned with growth. I had heard Garry talk about their plan design over the years. An initial conversation with Garry led us to working directly with Stan. Over the past two years of working together, the ideas refined and implemented by Garry and Stan have made a profound difference at Blanchard.

My father has consistently said two things: life is a journey, not a destination, *and* life is what happens when you are planning on doing something else. In the partnership between Garry and Stan both ideas have intersected wonderfully. Twenty-five years ago, Garry's life as a leader was transformed by many of the ideas he learned from my dad and his colleagues. Garry then spent decades bringing these ideas to life, in practice at WD-40 Company, in partnership with Stan. Through their hard work, experimentation, mistakes and missteps (a.k.a. "learning moments"), Garry and Stan refined a method of building a strong and resilient culture aligned around values, purpose and growth which have proven to be incredibly successful in a global, public company.

In this book you will find an inspired and practical guide to creating a world class, highly engaged culture that is resilient, aligned, sustainable and built for growth.

Scott Blanchard

INTRODUCTION

There are many books about building a strong culture in a business. Why did I add to the pile, you might ask? A story is in order.

When I started my first company, HRG Inc., I did so out of necessity. I had been fired from my role at a biotech startup after two years there. The reason was really that I didn't fit in the culture; my values and those of senior leaders were not congruent. It was just a few months after I refused to fire an accountant because he was gay that my boss, the CEO, asked to meet with me, then began the conversation with, "I don't know how to start these things…". He proceeded to tell me that I was being let go.

That was March of 1989, at the beginning of a recession. There were no jobs to be had in San Diego, which was reeling from the massive downturn in aerospace and defense caused by the collapse of the Soviet Union. Being unemployed was not a new experience for me. I'd been on my own since age 17 and had to find new work multiple times. But this was the first time I was out of a job as a father with a mortgage. I had two choices: take my family to a new city where there was better opportunity—or start a business. I chose the latter, and it was the best decision I have ever made professionally.

Since that time, I have founded a total of four companies: HRG (organizational consulting services), Emlyn Systems (HR database software), Chromagen (biotech diagnostics) and KI Investment Holdings (a private equity firm). In all these adventures, I endeavored to create organizations that had a higher purpose than just profit. I led with values first and believed that the financial results would be more likely positive with those values. While not all my entrepreneurial adventures were financially successful, all of them had meaning and purpose that made the dedication of my life to the work worthwhile.

One of my long-standing consulting clients was WD-40 Company. Early in 2012, when the private equity business was fully invested, I planned on cutting back my work hours. Concurrent with the private equity effort, I had been continuing as an advisor to a group of clients that I had come to know and value deeply. In January of 2012 I was working with Garry and the European leadership of WD-40 Company at a strategic planning meeting in London. At the end of the meetings, Garry and I shared a steak and ale pie, and a couple of pints at the King's Arms in Shepherd Market. When our mugs were half empty, Garry said to me, "Stan, what if you came to work at WD-40 Company?" By that time, I had been an entrepreneur for about 23 years, and was not even thinking about being an "employee" again. I asked him, "Do you mean part-time?" He said "no". I told Garry that I didn't know how to be an employee anymore. He said, "I don't need an employee. I need a business partner."

WD-40 Company was the only organization I had encountered in my time as a business owner and serial entrepreneur which I felt was approaching the conduct of business in the same fashion that I had been, i.e., putting values above everything else. I had worked with over 1,200 businesses by that point in time, from nearly every industry. No other client came close to the positive culture Garry was leading. I had personally witnessed Garry himself uphold the values of his company even when it was financially harmful for the business, and when it was specifically harmful to his own compensation. Garry was the only client who ever asked me, "Stan, how can we become a better client for you and your firm?"

Helping Garry and the rest of the leaders at WD-40 Company navigate the organizational development and change that was coming seemed like the right thing to do at that stage in my life. WD-40 Company was, to me, a noble experiment in humanistic capitalism that deserved to advance. So, I accepted the role of VP Global Organization Development, which was the HR leadership role. My purpose was to help the company prepare for its next sixty years (as it was 60 years old when I joined). My foundational motto upon assuming my role was "World peace through lubrication." I reasoned that if this multi-national organization—comprised of people from all walks of life, languages, politics, and religions—could create a unified tribe of like-minded people working together with common values to achieve great things, then there was hope for the world in general.

The usual friction that exists between people inside companies that do not focus on optimizing the human experience creates all the damage that friction inflicts on moving parts in any mechanical device. How beautiful the simile, that WD-40 Company's culture and values act on the organization just like its flagship product does on equipment—things run smoother, resist corrosion, need fewer repairs, and last longer.

What was anticipated to be a 3 to 5-year stint turned into nine. I retired from WD-40 Company in January of 2021. Then the company returned to being a client. I now work occasionally with its leaders as invited in a variety of areas, including leadership coaching and development, compensation strategy and supporting the ESG program, which I led prior to my retirement. I also work with other CEOs and business owners, all of whom wish to improve their organizational culture, their engagement level, and their performance.

Back to the question of "Why write this book?" Having not only been a student of positive, engaged organizational culture creation, but also a person who has bet his own time, talent, and significant treasure on these concepts, I saw a gap in the available information for business owners and leaders who want to accomplish the same things that WD-40 Company's leaders have. There isn't much out there that talks about the specifics of *how* to build a great culture where people want to stay and work hard towards common goals, with common values. There isn't a culture Rosetta Stone that decently translates "People, Purpose, Profits", for example, into methods, decisions, and actions. I began exploring the idea of creating a conference where CEOs could come to find out more about the "How to", not just the "Why should I?"

The result has been a partnership of Garry, me, Davin Salvagno (CEO and Founder of Purpose Point) and Dr. Chamu Sundaramurthy (professor of strategy and prior Chair of the Management Department at San Diego State University's Fowler College of Business) to create the Culture Forum, which will have its inaugural event at San Diego State University on October 24 and 25, 2023. This conference is designed to go deeper than the surface discussions or the inspirational keynotes. The conference will dig into the mechanics of building a positive culture "engine" that sustainably creates a highly engaged, coherent group of people, guided by values, achieving a larger purpose as well as a financial result that sustains the people and their stakeholders.

There will be a variety of viewpoints offered on the "How to" at our Culture Forum. That's a good thing. Leaders must be broadly informed, skeptical, and judicious about what they decide to implement towards their goal of achieving high engagement and an enduringly positive organizational culture.

I am writing this book as an adjunct to the conference, so that the information I feel is important, but which couldn't fit into the two days of our Culture Forum, can still be accessed by the attendees, and by anyone else who is interested. What I've included is my opinion, based on the experiences I've had.

I am not a notable "thought leader". I don't get paid for speaking engagements. You won't find me on anyone's list of top coaches, entrepreneurs, or culture experts. But what you will read here is based on my ongoing education and decades of experience as a business owner and leader. I am sharing what I personally know has worked, to create and sustain the kind of organization I wanted to be a part of. I've experienced these principles operating effectively across industries, national boundaries, diverse political structures, languages, religions, and all other distinguishing factors that otherwise would seem to separate people. I'm not saying I know all the answers. I just know *my* answers.

Many of the case examples I employ are from WD-40 Company, based on my experiences having worked with Garry and other leaders over a 22-year period. I also draw on experiences from my own companies and others with whom I have personal knowledge.

I invite you to take issue with any of it, truly. I'm still learning; this is what I've concluded so far. You must decide your own views, of course.

A caveat of importance: I am no longer an employee of the company. These are my perspectives, and do not necessarily represent those of the company's current leadership. The practices I describe from my time with the company may have evolved or might in the future.

One other thing. This book is being written as if I'm speaking to a CEO or President, which is the person I hope is reading it. Very little can happen towards creating a positive, engaged culture that is values-driven and successful unless the CEO *and* their senior leaders set the example. I will be beating that drum throughout the book. But it's a fact. As I used to say when people would thank me for some aspect of WD-40 Company's people-centered methods, "Don't thank me. Nothing would have happened without Garry".

WHAT IS "ENGAGEMENT"?

The Gallup organization has done annual or biennial surveys on this subject for quite some time. The results in the U.S. are fairly consistent—no more than a third of employees feel "engaged" at work. The rest are either not engaged or "actively disengaged", which means they are applying effort in *opposition* to the company's objectives.

The best definition of "engagement" I've seen is when a person continually applies discretionary effort above and beyond what is being asked of them. An engaged person wants to be part of the organization, feels a responsibility for its success and the success of everyone around them. They feel like they belong, are respected, and valued. They go out of their way to contribute, to help others.

At WD-40 Company, a formal global engagement survey is conducted every two years, and sometimes during the intervening years when it is important to get input from the tribe. Since inception of the survey process in 2000, the average overall engagement has been 91%, through 2022, with a consistently high level of participation at about 97% of the company population. Since 2006 engagement has averaged 93%. This means that on average 93% of the people responded "agree" or "strongly agree" to a set of statements related to the factors that cause people to feel "engaged". And 98% of

WD-40 Company's tribe members say that they "love to tell people they work for WD-40 Company".

The 26 queries of the Engagement Survey comprise six personal experience factors. These factors were selected because they have been consistently shown to directly correlate to people being more engaged in their organizations. And they make perfect sense. Here they are:

- **Optimism about the future, for the company and for themselves**
  If people feel confident that the organization is headed in the right direction and the prospects for the company are good, they will feel safer and more comfortable in continuing to commit their life and effort to it.

  If people feel that their own career aspirations can be satisfied within the organization, they have less motivation to make a change, and are more likely to apply strong effort.

  If a person is worried about whether they will be laid off, they will focus their attention on opportunities outside the company and reserve application of effort, saving their energy to prepare for the possibility of being out of a job. Without a sense of personal safety, people won't think long-term about their work and their impact.

  As CEO, what is *your* level of optimism about your own future? How long do you wish to serve as CEO in your company? According to an article written in 2019 in the Harvard Business Review, "The CEO Life Cycle" (James M. Citrin, Claudius A. Hildebrand and Robert J. Stark), a study of 747 CEOs in the S&P 500 showed that the average tenure was 7.2 years, but that the average tenure of the best-performing CEOs was double that, at 15 years. (Garry Ridge served WD-40 Company 35 years, with 25 of them as CEO.)

If a CEO only envisions a tenure for themselves of the average seven years, because they want to step "up" to a CEO position in a larger company with higher pay, for example, they won't be that interested in embarking upon an initiative or strategic path that will take ten to fifteen years to accomplish. If you are CEO of a public company and you are focused on quarter-to-quarter performance, concerned about your board's confidence in you, what is your planning horizon?

If you are the owner, or at least majority stockholder, you have the luxury of being secure in your role. But even public company CEOs can learn to lead with a telescope rather than a microscope. I saw that first-hand with Garry Ridge. The point is, you can't expect your organization's people to think and act with a ten or twenty-year mindset if you are working with a quarterly or yearly perspective yourself.

- **Meaning of their work**
  People need an emotional connection with their work and their company. Serving a purpose that is larger than themselves, larger than the products or services offered, brings with it a deep satisfaction. If it's only about profits, the work becomes hollow. There's no feeling to create glue between the company and the person.

Everyone who works for a living brings a larger purpose with them, if only to earn that living for themselves and anyone else they support. Then they discover whether the organization they've joined has an over-arching purpose that is additionally meaningful to them. If that is indeed the case, the bond created is strong and can survive periodic challenges of difficult times, or solicitations from other employers.

Meaning of the work is an inherent motivator, as opposed to external motivators like compensation, benefits and pats on the back. As research has shown, inherent motivators are more enduring and resilient than external motivators (but which are also important).

Many companies spend a lot of time with consultants, internal focus groups and marketing experts to come up with their purpose and vision. This can be fruitful, and it can also be just surface activity with no foundational substance. There's a difference between establishing a brand message for a company or a product and articulating the emotional reason for being in business at all. Above all, the effort to establish meaningful purpose must be authentic.

I participated in an organization called Conscious Capitalism for several years. It's a group of business leaders and owners who worked together to pursue what I call "humanistic capitalism", i.e., capitalism that serves the organization's people in total, including both economic health and quality of life. Occasionally a business owner or leader would join, because they were curious about the subject and wanted to explore the improved results that can come with a positive, engaged group of people.

At one meeting a restauranteur who was in the early stages of expanding through franchises said that he had taken the first steps to forming a company purpose by meeting with everyone in the company to get their ideas. Heads nodded around the conference table. I asked him what he learned from those discussions. He couldn't come up with anything definitive, saying that the notes were taken by his assistant. I said to him, "If you can't remember what you heard, you weren't listening with the intent to be influenced. The effect will be worse than if you hadn't asked them at all. They will feel like they wasted their time and that you don't really care. *Do* you really care?" He didn't return to the next meeting.

Forming your purpose is not a marketing project. It's not a technique to manipulate people to increase their contributions. It starts with your own authentic self-awareness and then must be joined by willing participants who are also inspired to help define the purpose that is heartfelt and true.

- **Relationship with their immediate coach (their supervisor or manager)**
  If a person knows that their immediate leader cares about them and is actively working to help them succeed, now and in the future, then they are much more likely to want to stay and devote strong effort. If their leader treats them with respect, as a valued member of the organization, they have little reason to want to leave.

Showing respect includes telling someone the truth, caring enough about them to provide honest input on their abilities and their areas that need to be developed.

As it has been said, people don't leave a company as much as they leave a poor relationship with their leader.

In the Leadership Lab course at WD-40 Company that introduced the topic of leadership to participants, we would discuss the behaviors that increase the mutual respect between a leader and those led. We would ask the workshop attendees to list the qualities and characteristics they wanted to see in their leaders. This has been done countless times in research projects that study leadership. The list is consistently the same, no matter who you ask, what year you ask them, what age they are or what position they hold. People want their leaders to be capable, confident, caring, honest, selfless, clear, humble, hard-working, able to make good decisions, and devoted to helping people succeed. Living up to that list is the challenge.

- **Influence over the work they do**
  Autonomy is a key inherent motivator for most people. Being trusted and respected to decide how to accomplish one's responsibilities, and the freedom to choose, is one of the primary reasons why people engage strongly in their work.

  Perceived micro-management and tight confinement of allowable methods feels like running a race with ankle weights, especially as a person increases their skills, their competencies.

Sometimes, autonomy can be scary, however. If a person is left to figure something out on their own that they have never done before, without any guidance or education, it can have the exact opposite effect. When and how to apply the right delegatory approach is a skill leaders must acquire to ensure autonomy is indeed motivating.

It should be noted here that no one learns how to do something well until after they have done it a while. The first time you became a CEO, you were a novice in that role. Everyone who takes on a new role is a beginner, no matter how many years they have spent in preparation. It's always different when you're actually in the seat.

Trusting someone to learn through their successes and mistakes, erring to the side of delegation and allowing them freedom to choose how to accomplish their goals, is the only path to truly developing talent. It's highly motivating to the person being trusted.

- **Their sense of belonging**
  If someone feels included, welcome and even celebrated by their colleagues and leaders, the emotional bond grows strong, which results in higher contributions and longevity in tenure.

But is everyone invited to everything? Stratification of accountability is a reality in how businesses organize and lead the work to be done. It's the only efficient way to allocate time, the most precious resource. While such distinctions are practical and necessary, if people feel that they have *access* to anyone, no matter what "level" in the company they occupy, then they don't resent the hierarchy of authority. They don't feel excluded from important relationships.

The superficial physical distinctions that people often use to separate and categorize each other are impediments to collective, effective, cohesive action. They reduce the creativity and resourcefulness of a group because they cause fragmentation in communication and action. I'm speaking practically, not politically. Being inclusive creates a better-performing organization with less interpersonal friction, less conflict, more cohesion, more resilience. If the primary method of distinguishing whether someone is "in" or "out" is whether they live the values, contribute to accomplishing goals and how they treat each other, then the criteria for inclusion are aligned with a culture of high engagement.

You know you are achieving a culture of inclusion and belonging when people say things like, "I can be myself here."

- **Alignment with the company's values and purpose**
  When there is congruency between a person's individual ethics and values, and the company's lived values (how people daily behave), personal commitment grows, and efforts are strong to ensure the organization succeeds. It matters to people.

  When the organizational purpose is emotionally compelling, the values are felt to be pointed towards a future and vision that is larger than one person, and worth pursuing.

However, if people feel that the real purpose of the organization is solely to benefit a small group of people, or only for shareholders, it is difficult for them to see a reason why they should contribute more than what is asked. Their relationship with the company becomes strictly transactional. Now it's a contest of "fairness" of balance between paid work and what the person would rather be doing, i.e., "work-life balance".

When I am speaking with someone who is not happy with their "work-life balance", it often is caused by a feeling of not being connected to the organizational values and purpose. They are not happy to devote time beyond the minimum expectations, because there isn't enough reason to.

Study after study has solidified these six factors as the critical elements of creating high engagement. These factors are the categories of intentional actions that leaders must take to positively affect collective engagement. Disconnection in any one of them can be a powerful source of erosion of the organization's culture.

There's your roadmap. Pay attention to each and every factor, making progress to achieve high marks from your people. Your culture will thrive.

Simple? Yes. Easy? Not on your life. Nothing worthwhile is, though, right?

The rest of this book addresses the leadership principles and methods you and your leaders can adopt, directly related to these six factors of human experience, to achieve the kind of culture that people love to be a part of.

MEASURING ENGAGEMENT

Surveying employees through an anonymous online tool is important to assess the state of mind of people and get information about trends, when the population is too large for you to interact with regularly as CEO. It's a primary way leadership can get a more direct, comprehensive view as the organization expands its population and geographic locations. But it has certain sources of error that should be kept in mind.

One error source is that not everyone tells the truth when they provide their ratings and comments. They may be afraid to say what they really think for fear of some type of retribution, even if there has never been any negative leadership reaction to the input received. And if their own direct leader tends to react angrily to any type of criticism of their leadership, the survey will be similarly viewed as a dangerous place to tell the truth. Therefore, some percentage of people, hopefully small, will distrust that the survey input is anonymous, no matter how much you try to show them the proof.

If you do such a survey and state that it's anonymous, but then you actually open the hood to find out who said what, that will become known, and you will not have any chance of getting honest input—or much input at all—from any future survey efforts. Different survey tools have varying functionality about anonymity, with some having the capability of reversing the confidentiality feature. It's best to have the survey administered by an external service provider, to further prove the fact of anonymity.

Another source of error is the rate of participation. At WD-40 Company, only a few percent typically failed to respond, and the biggest reason was that they were on some sort of leave during the survey period. If the rate of absent respondents reaches even 10%, it can create significantly inaccurate results. Generally, low participation translates to low engagement by those deciding to ignore the request to participate.

What you do with the information gained is critical. At WD-40 Company, senior leadership reviewed the results of the entire company as well as each sub-division, e.g., trading bloc, country and functional department. With a high overall engagement score of 93% you might think that deep analysis might not be necessary. Just the opposite is true. Having a high score is like holding a package of cheese that nicely fills out the envelope. It looks solid. Until you cut it open and realize it's Swiss. You must pay attention to the holes.

Each trading bloc saw the overall company ratings and their trading bloc. Each country additionally viewed their specific results. If a functional group had less than 7 people, those results were included in the next larger reporting segment, such as broader functional category, country or trading bloc. This helped protect anonymity as well.

Senior leadership met to discuss the results across the company, determine what issues appeared to be important, and begin forming actions to address lower scoring segments.

Some actions took months, and some took years to show progress in improving responses for a particular question.

Any score of less than or equal to 80% agree/strongly agree on a given query was a warning light. Any score of less than 70% was a fire siren. I know organizations that would love to have engagement as high as 70%, and they are working on it. But the higher you achieve, the more important it is to focus on both improvement and not missing the alarm bells that engagement may have slid, or specific groups were in trouble.

The open-ended queries are critical. While the ratings are informative about sentiment trends, the gold is in the comments. This is where you hear, in the respondent's own words, what was top of mind for them in terms of what needed to improve, and suggestions on how to do so. The comments also showed what people truly valued specifically and what they thought should continue, in the six domains of queries. The depth of detail provided showed how much they cared about the culture and preserving it. No edits were made to the commentary unless what was written could identify themselves or someone else as associated with the input. Such identifying wording was adjusted to preserve anonymity.

We chose to do the survey every two years. One reason is that some of the actions implemented to positively affect engagement took significant time to put in operation. Another reason was that it's possible to over-ask. If every year you are requested to do the same survey, and possibly additional surveys for other purposes as well, the frequency can reach the point where another invitation to describe one's opinion starts to feel like those incessant requests to do product and service reviews on Yelp. Certainly, the weekly "pings" that some culture-sensing online applications offer will be useless after a few months.

Another source of error that may enter the analysis is when people may have a "halo" effect regarding their opinions and perceptions. If engagement is steadily high for a period of years, some people don't want to give a lower response than they did for the prior surveys. They explain away their critical opinion or don't want to "disappoint" a leader whom they cherish and respect. Again, that is why the written commentary will tell you more than a possibly elevated rating.

In smaller functional groups of 7 to 10 or so, some people will worry about anonymity and so they may hold back their true feelings for fear of being sought out personally. Even if there is no evidence of any retribution for being critically honest, it is human nature (for a lot of folks) to avoid a confrontation about their negative perceptions. Such respondents may at times seek to homogenize their input with others: "What did you put down for number 14?" Or they will simply honey-cut their answer.

With these sources of error, I recommend you take off a few points from whatever overall results you obtain for your engagement survey. It's better to assume a little lower score than make the error of believing all the good news at its highest interpretation. By doing so you will be more diligent in your ongoing efforts to lead in a manner that improves engagement.

The size of a survey is a key design element. We originally had over 100 questions in the survey. In 2014 we reduced it to 26 well-crafted, potent queries, spread across the six factors, while maintaining the key questions from the prior version correlated to engagement. This dramatically reduced survey fatigue and increased the volume of valuable open-ended comments we received.

We also increased the difficulty of obtaining an "agree" or "strongly agree" response, by combining conditions in some of the queries. For example, one query was to respond with level of agreement to this statement: "I consider my immediate supervisor both a mentor and a coach". They are not the same. Our aspiration was that leaders could be effective as both, which would be deeply impactful to someone's sense of engagement. Another statement of the survey was "I love to tell people I work for WD-40 Company." Not "like", not "I enjoy working here". When people truly love to tell others about their place of work, it is a high endorsement for the organization, a point of pride and confirmation of belonging. That's a high bar to shoot for. Therefore, our engagement measure got harder to achieve high scoring after we modified it, and our overall score remained a bit over 93%.

Surveys are an important tool, but only one tool, and much less powerful as an organizational diagnostic than open, trusting, candid communication between leaders and those led. Sometimes organizations rely on the survey process to gauge employee attitudes, and reduce the attention that leaders devote to really knowing the people who rely on them, what they truly think. It's a natural tendency in general to try to make leadership "more efficient" by depending on surveys or other self-report assessments to short-cut the process of understanding the minds of the people in your organization.

I have found there is no better way of gaining true understanding of someone's perceptions and experiences than taking the time to build open, honest relationships. The tools, engagement surveys included, are additional supports, not replacements, for leaders being personally engaged with those for whom they are accountable.

Other indicators of engagement aside from surveys are helpful as well. For example, analyzing turnover can offer clues. Measuring new employee turnover (one, two and three-years after hire) will provide an indicator of how well you are evaluating candidates comprehensively and how well they are being led after they joined. Understanding why candidates decline offers is another source of information.

The incidence rate of interpersonal conflicts and performance counseling events can reveal systemic human dynamics that can erode engagement. How many people are taking advantage of development opportunities, such as leadership education or voluntary assignments, is another indicator. Whether people show up for celebrations or honoring their colleagues can be a sign. How someone perceives their coach's relationship with senior leaders will be an indicator of how positive they should feel about their own relationships. In other words, it all matters and you must pay attention to all the signals.

As CEO, these methods of evaluating engagement are important to you. With time you will develop an internal "radar" that is attuned to the cultural behavioral cues if you make a point of interacting with a broad range of people in your organization, not just your senior leaders.

VALUES COME FIRST, THEN PURPOSE

The public literature is full of discussion and articles about organizational values. It's a popular topic, because it has become widely accepted that people connect more with each other and with their employers if they share common ethical and moral guideposts. Sharing deeper principles of life creates a strong link between people and a sense of mutual support. It's a tribal feeling.

Garry brought the concept of "tribe" to WD-40 Company. He grew up in Australia and learned something of the aboriginal people who had lived for eons there before Europeans "discovered" the huge island, a common colonial theme around the world at that time. As he studied what it meant to be a tribe, the attributes rang true to his vision of the kind of culture he wanted to create.

Tribal elders are learners and teachers. Celebrations and customs connect people. The tribe represents an extension of a sense of family and belonging. Your tribe is the collection of people who you will help feed and defend. Tribes celebrate together. They mourn each other's losses together. Tribes have a code of conduct that they establish, shared principles of how to behave with integrity.

Even if you don't write them down, your "code of conduct", i.e., your values, still exist. Even if you don't communicate them to the rest of the organization, people will watch what you do and emulate you. If what you say and what you do are not congruent, you can bet people will do what you do, not what you say. If they stay, that is.

So, what are the values that you, as CEO, want to guide your business and your personal actions? What values will you live by even to the detriment of profit or your own personal comfort?

This is not a trivial exercise and cannot be done in a vacuum. Handing out a list of values you've composed to the employees in your company won't embed them into the hearts and minds of everyone in the organization. People may say they are aligned with your values, but in truth they may only tolerate them while they quietly follow their own hearts.

Consciously engaging people in the design and definition of the values that your organization will embody, and will place above all other objectives, is a methodical process that cannot be cut short. It takes time and it takes authentic engagement between you as CEO and everyone else who will be part of the work.

To start, you must look in the mirror. Ask yourself:

- "What do I stand for?"
- "What ethics and principles of life will I follow, even if by doing so I suffer personally?"

- "What behavior do I want to demonstrate, even to the detriment of revenue, profit, business valuation and personal wealth?"

In other words, what is more important to you than money, fame, prestige, or personal comfort?

It has been said that "everyone has a price", meaning that everyone will subordinate their stated values at a certain monetary level of inducement. If one of your values is integrity—defined as being honest, trustworthy, congruent in word and deed—would you lie or cheat in exchange for a payment of $100 million dollars? How about $1 billion?

If you don't remember the Enron fiasco, or haven't read about it, it would be instructive to study that example of people having a price at which their ethics are subordinated. The complex entity structure Enron employed went far beyond simply stretching the bounds of propriety, and it allowed the company to present a valuation to the public and shareholders that was based on accounting sleight of hand, even though its method was approved by the SEC. Enron had a partner in this subterfuge. Arthur Andersen was the accounting firm Enron hired to audit the books and present an opinion as to whether shareholders and the public could rely on the financial reports of the company to represent the company's state accurately and fairly. Andersen's legal advisors told the firm to destroy its Enron files just a few months before the crap hit the public fan. Andersen was forced to dissolve itself as a result of the legal action taken and is no more.

An irony of Andersen's demise is that all those accountants who were let go when the accounting firm closed its doors went to the other four remaining large accounting companies (and to smaller firms) which had to pick up all the clients that Andersen previously served. This caused accounting fees to go up dramatically because there were fewer competitors vying for the same number of clients.

Enron and Arthur Andersen (along with some other contemporary notable lapses of corporate integrity) caused the political will to pass significant legislation, called the Sarbanes-Oxley Act, which slapped a lot more regulatory oversight onto all public companies. The four remaining big accounting firms now had a lucrative new service to offer, i.e., helping their public clients to install and operate the broad range of procedural requirements to be compliant with the new law that was significantly caused by one of their own. And service fees went up again.

So, the accounting profession, if not Arthur Andersen specifically, was actually *rewarded* for the massive lapse of ethics that Andersen and its client, Enron, demonstrated.

I raise this example to demonstrate that having values is continually and powerfully tested by temptation of significant monetary rewards that can be achieved through having no values or having situational values (those that change in varying circumstances).

More recent examples of how money has trumped ethics are numerous, from the Theranos debacle to the world of crypto currencies, to fraudulent use of Paycheck Protection Program funds during the pandemic, to…well, you read the headlines as well as I.

But what about you? Do your principles cease after a certain financial number? I am pretty certain the answer is "no", or you would not have picked up this book.

If you believe that your values are indeed worth paying for then they are truly your values. Because values are only real if they do cost you at times to keep them. If you haven't yet had to "pay" to hold onto your values, you will be tested at some point, like I was when the biotech company CFO wanted me to fire an accountant for being gay. And that's when you will find out if you really have values, or you don't.

Assuming you do think (or know) that your values are bedrock, foundational principles by which you live, the next step in creating shared values in your organization is engaging others in exploring them as a basis for expectations of behavior of everyone in your company.

So how do you do that?

The first time I consciously addressed values in my own business was 1992. I had founded a consulting firm in 1989, as I mentioned in the introduction. I had created the business plan three years earlier, but I wouldn't have jumped off the diving board if somebody hadn't pushed me off. I had previously thought it was too big a risk for my family.

I could have either left town to find work in an area that wasn't as hard hit after the fall of the Iron Curtain, or I could become a white belt entrepreneur. I had enough funds saved and available through a line of credit to last a year. My reasoning was that if I got to the six-month mark, and still had a year of financing remaining, then I'd keep going. If I didn't have the year ahead covered, I'd look for another job, and likely need to move my family.

After a few years, continuing to test that one-year rule, the business was starting to grow. I paid off the debt I used to launch the company, had employees, was growing largely through referrals and the future looked brighter. I wanted to be intentional about what kind of organization I wanted to create, because my experiences in "Corporate Land" prior to that point were less than inspiring. I wanted to build a place where people wanted to be, where teamwork was exciting and fun. I wanted to create an organization where both strong performance and a high quality of life could exist together. I called it "humanistic capitalism".

As the leader of your company, you must start with your own values. You'll discover if others are attracted to them, and whether their values are those that you would want to add to your own list.

I first wrote down descriptions of how I wanted to experience my work life.

I then met with my team and shared the drafted values. I asked, "Do these describe the kind of company you want to be a part of?"

We had multiple meetings, with honest and deep dialogue. The people in HRG Inc. at that time had not experienced anything like what we were doing. The exercise alone was a way of drawing us closer together as human beings. When we finished, we were satisfied that the values we created together were shared, deeply desired and were more important than anything else about our business. In other words, if we had to give up our values in order to make money, we'd rather give up the money.

Here are the values we settled on at HRG:

- We care as much about each other as we do about ourselves.
- We are a team. We look for opportunities to contribute to each other's success, as well as to the success of the entire company. We think "we" before "I".
- We believe in and strive for the growth of HRG, Inc.
- We respect each other as people and as colleagues. This includes privacy: asking permission before we interrupt, intrude, or assume. We allow ourselves and others the license to say, "not now", when quality of our work would suffer.
- We look for the opportunity to take responsibility and give credit, rather than the reverse.
- We bring up "touchy" subjects quickly and squarely, and we resolve them. We know that this isn't always a comfortable process.
- We seek out personal growth and stretch ourselves daily. We value growth over comfort. We value experience over luxury.
- We know when it's time to hone existing skills and not stretch too fast or too far.
- We continually strive for learning.
- We are self-sufficient as much as possible, and we ask for help before it's too late.
- We take intelligent risks, and we accept that our best can sometimes fail. We don't repeat mistakes.

- We all make coffee, take messages, clean our own mugs, run errands, move furniture, and fill the staplers.
- We have a good measure of fun.
- This culture is real and living. It is not just paper on a wall.

You'll notice that these culture statements, as we called them at the time, did not include anything about our clients. These were more about how we would interact and behave within our company. We had other principles that we applied to our business activities, such as guaranteeing our work unconditionally. If a client was dissatisfied with the service they received, we would provide a refund and cancel outstanding invoices upon request, no questions asked.

Values in your organization are not just the words you put on a list of characteristics. There are other values you and your leaders exhibit without having focus groups about the topic. Like quality of work, being direct and honest in communications or helping each other without having to be asked. These leadership behaviors also convey the values of an organization. Not every value appears on the wall, but demonstrated character is displayed everywhere and thus reveals the broad range of values you as a leader advertise.

We had a great team at HRG, at least those who stayed. I made a few hiring mistakes. Some people just weren't aligned with our values. And some people were aligned with the values but couldn't do the kind of work we did. Consulting is a very tough profession if it's done well. You are hand-crafting intellectual services that must be the absolute best. Your client's business sometimes depends upon that guidance.

As we used to remind ourselves, our clients didn't come to us with the easy problems.

Eight years after HRG composed its values, in 2001, we acquired a new client: WD-40 Company. The HR leader at that time was someone we had gotten to know when recruiting for a client. She was one of the candidates for a senior HR role that we had interviewed. She felt respected and treated well during our interviewing process. She appreciated our thorough approach to evaluating a person's match to a role. So, she called us to help with improving WD-40 Company's compensation system and providing leadership coaching to their leaders.

After some time working closely with this phenomenal company, I became Garry's coach. Garry was five years into his tenure leading the company, at the time I began working directly with him. Our relationship evolved in this manner. We'd be talking, he'd ask a question related to a dilemma of leadership he was facing, I'd offer ideas which he found effective, and we just continued from there.

To that point, as I said, I had not encountered another company other than my own, which had placed values above all else. That included hundreds and hundreds of clients. Not until WD-40 Company did I experience another organization who seemed to believe the way I did, about how to create a positive environment. One day, Garry asked me if I could help in the process of improving the values adopted by the company. The values at that time were brief phrases without explanation. Many companies approach their values in this way, often as a list of nouns that are open for interpretation: "Integrity", "Creativity", "Teamwork", "Ingenuity", etc.

Garry wanted to go deeper. And he wanted to involve as many people as he could. That would be no small task, with employees spread thin and wide around the world.

We convened leadership meetings on the subject. We sent out the draft values to every employee, translated into the local languages of the country where they worked. We gathered all the input and then met again with the senior leadership team. I took the value statements and drafted descriptions of the behavior that should be observed if those values were being "lived" and not just "visited". Those descriptions were circulated widely, edited from input received, repeatedly polished until there were no more suggestions.

It took a year, folding the work into the ongoing daily priorities of the company, to arrive at the completed values and their operational definitions—the behaviors that showed they were being exhibited. It was very important to illustrate examples of what it meant to live by a value. Without the descriptive behavioral definitions, there would be too much room for interpretation that would result in gradual deflection of behavior away from the intended result, or lack of understanding of what the value meant.

Aside from a small addition of illustrative language a few years ago for one specific value, these descriptions have stood the test of time and remain the enduring, guiding values that, in Garry's words, "protect people and set them free". Meaningful, shared values allow people to make daily decisions related to their work, to decide how to interact, without the need for lots of policy manuals and rules.

Completed in 2006, these values continued to guide the company's tribe daily. That is not an exaggeration. Every quarterly performance discussion includes how the person has demonstrated behaviors that show they have "lived" the values. Every business decision of significance is evaluated not only on the financial or strategic impacts, but first on the alignment to the values. Leadership education workshops on strategic thinking include the values as a business tool to evaluate various actions and initiatives. Contracting with vendors includes an assessment of values alignment. Relationships with external partners are continued or severed, depending upon whether doing so would be in accordance with the company's values. Candidates for open roles are assessed on character match to the values. The values are applied literally everywhere, every day.

If you don't apply your carefully composed and jointly adopted organizational values to make business decisions, to make people decisions and to establish the expected behaviors within the company, they end up being that pretty, hypocritical piece of paper on the wall. It is worse for an organization to adopt a set of values and not live them, than it is to not have any consciously adopted and stated values at all.

Following are WD-40 Company's six values as of this writing (there's always the possibility of evolution). Note that they are in hierarchical order of priority. It is not always possible to achieve all the values at the same time, although that is the goal. As you can see, the economic value is the last one. We reasoned that if we adhered to the first five, which were more important than financial results, number six would be much more likely achieved anyway:

"We value doing the right thing."

"We do the right thing in serving our tribe, our stockholders, our customers, our products, our end-users, our suppliers and even our competitors. This means looking for the right action in every context and asking critical questions that bring out the best course or decisions relevant to the situation and the circumstances. It also means being honest in both word and deed. Being reliable, dependable, and competent. And doing what's right according to the situation and the context. If we are honest and we speak and act congruently, we will be doing what is right."

"We value creating positive lasting memories in all our relationships."

"As a result of our interactions with our tribe and stakeholders, we all will feel better at the end of the interaction than we did when we began; we will leave with a positive memory of it. Our stockholders should be proud to say they own our stock. Our customers should consider us a part of their business success. End-users should be glad they purchased our products, telling their friends about the quality and utility of our brands. Our company name and our many brands should become known as emblems of quality, performance, and value. Our tribe members should consider each other valued friends and colleagues who share work, struggles, successes, life, and laughter over the years. If we successfully live these values, the result will be a higher degree of mutual trust and respect."

"We value making it better than it is today."

"We value continual improvement. We are a learning organization. We are responsible for our own development and helping others to learn, as well. We celebrate our successes, then move on to new heights of achievement. We solicit ideas and solutions from all, and consistently look for ways to progress. We are comfortable with self-criticism and receiving constructive feedback. We take the time to recognize others who do the same. We endeavor not to repeat mistakes. We value the development of our people in order to enhance their skills and to improve their career opportunities. There is a special moment which occurs right at the point in time where a person gains an insight or new knowledge because of a particularly positive...or negative...event. We are constantly on the lookout for these 'learning moments' because they are the fuel for continual improvement."

"We value succeeding as a tribe while excelling as individuals."

"We recognize that collective success comes first. Our organization is a global company with many different locations and tribe members spread far and wide. But everything we do is geared toward the success of the entire company. And within the company are smaller groups, whether they are functional departments or teams defined by geography. The same philosophy applies in these sub-teams. We believe the individual can't 'win' at the expense of, or apart from, the tribe. But individual excellence is the means by which our organization succeeds. And 'excellence' is defined as outstanding contribution to the whole. Our mantra is one world, one company, one tribe."

"We value owning it and passionately acting on it."

"We get our shoes dirty. We are relentless about understanding our business and our role in impacting it. We are passionate about our end users, customers, and markets, and how we can positively impact them. We act in ways that maintain our traditions while positioning us powerfully for the future. We consider carefully, act boldly, and course correct as needed."

"We value sustaining the WD-40 Company economy."

"We realize creating and protecting economic value for our tribe and its stakeholders is a tremendous responsibility. We take seriously the fact that many families are dependent upon the actions we take. We recognize and accept this responsibility."

At WD-40 Company, until 2017, the values were not actually displayed anywhere. But they were included in performance review forms. There were little wallet-sized cards with the values and their descriptions on them. We didn't need them on the wall because they were inside every person.

When the company moved to a new headquarters building in August of 2017, we finally put them up in the large conference room, which was used for educational workshops and business meetings. I was a bit superstitious about displaying the values in the conference room, concerned that once they were on the wall they might not reside in the hearts and minds of the tribe. My fears were unfounded, I am happy to report.

So here is your recipe for establishing the values in your organization:

1. List your own values, which should include descriptive behavioral language so you can know it when you see it (or don't).
2. Engage your leadership team to explore the list, making additions and adjustments that do not compromise your own values, but can be additive and more comprehensive.
3. Involve the entire company to review the drafted values, offering their reactions, comments, suggestions, additions and possible changes.
4. Convene your leadership team to review all the input. Try to include additional ideas offered that are not in contradiction with the values you crafted, and that are aligned with the overall culture you wish to create.
5. Distribute the next version to the entire company, asking for their level of agreement, and any further refinement that they think is important.
6. Keep iterating until you have at least 80% favoring adoption of the values composed. 90% or more is better.
7. Incorporate the values in how you make business decisions, how you evaluate candidates to hire, how you select people for promotion and how you evaluate employee performance. Establish the primacy of values in such evaluations, i.e., a person can't receive accolades for achieving goals and objectives while at the same time violating the values of the organization. Values trump performance.

The work is worth it. If done right, for the right reasons, you won't be revisiting your values every year. They will last a long, long time. Because true values are not situational. They don't depend on circumstances. They depend on you and your company's leaders behaving in accordance with them, every day. If leaders do, most everyone else will too.

Once you do have a clear set of values, with defined behaviors associated, now you can choose the purpose of your organization, if you haven't already. Think of the purpose as the direction your values will point towards. That purpose has to be enduringly true, independent of business models you might employ or even the specific products and services you offer your markets. The purpose must be larger than any one person, group, or segment. It must encompass everyone. The purpose must be connected to human motivations, which means the purpose must have an emotional context. It must *feel* right to the people working to fulfill it.

Here is WD-40 Company's purpose:

"We exist to create positive lasting memories in everything we do. We solve problems. We make things work smoothly. We create opportunities."

Listen to that first sentence. It is an alternate form of the second value of the company. Think about the implications. On a product level, if your consumers have a positive lasting memory because they use what you make, what are the odds they will purchase it again? How likely will they recommend it to someone else?

If you have positive lasting memories while working with your immediate manager and your colleagues, how satisfying do you think your daily life will be? How likely will you want to stay?

If you have positive lasting memories with your vendors and suppliers, what are the odds that you'll be able to retain those critical relationships through good times and bad? How much easier will it be to navigate the inevitable conflicts of interest that arise?

If people have great memories of the work they did together, the experiences they shared and the things they accomplished as a team, what are the odds they will want to continue having those experiences?

Achieving this purpose isn't easy, and not always possible. But perfection is not the goal. Continual improvement is.

Your values and your purpose, as initiated by you as CEO and co-created by your entire organization, can be the same or different than other organizations might choose. I've seen a fair amount of commonality across organizational values, and some interesting differences. There is no one set of values, or one purpose statement that is universal. I don't even think it is useful to do a broad scan of other samples from a lot of companies before you start. That approach could possibly confine your thinking and prevent you from discovering your authentic truth.

You might get some help arriving at your values and purpose, but really there's no magic process or "best practice" aside from pursuing an honest, transparent, collective exploration that you, as CEO, lead. All you need is a blank page and an engaged heart, to start.

IS YOUR BUSINESS HEALTHY?

Strong values and a clear purpose, both of which are attractive to the people you intend to invite to join you, are necessary to create the type of culture where people want to be, dedicating the time of their life. Necessary, but insufficient.

Equally important is the ability of your business to create economic opportunity that can be sustained over many years. I could have the best values and a great purpose, as a business owner. But if no customer wants what I provide, then there's little reason for people to dedicate their lives to my organization. Or if I cannot construct a strategy that produces growth and profitability, the business won't support the growth of the people within it.

This aspect of building a strong culture is sometimes lost in the popular discussion. Often, you'll hear the phrase, "Take care of your people and they'll take care of your customers. Your customers will take care of your profit." But this simple aphorism assumes you already have a strong customer base and the ability to generate revenue with good margins. What about a start-up? Or a new division within an existing company? What if the competitive dynamics change and a previously successful legacy business is threatened by substitutes? What if your business has been flat for several years with no ability to offer opportunities to the people within it? And even the most engaged organization on the planet might face an existential threat, regardless of the Herculean efforts the employees apply.

A key reason why WD-40 Company was able to dedicate many years to developing the kind of culture it has achieved to date is that the business model and strategies are sound. Most people know the company for its flagship multi-use product, found in nearly every household, factory and shop in the U.S. and many other countries. The company also has a wide range of other maintenance chemical products, as well as household care and cleaning products. These varied offerings were consciously created and strategically important to the growth of the company.

The strategy for expanding the geographic reach of the company's products was also carefully designed and meticulously executed, such that (at last count) WD-40 Company's products are being sold in 176 countries. The distributed, out-sourced supply chain model of fulfillment was another key strategic decision early in the company's history, which allowed efficient, flexible application of capital and capacity to meet demand, ever closer to the consumer's point of use.

My consulting business thrived for 23 years, in no small part because of the people who were truly engaged within it, but also because we provided needed services of high quality at attractive rates to market segments that were growing. The companies my private equity firm invested in, and which succeeded, had fundamentally solid economic theses. These business design elements were consciously and intentionally crafted.

This book isn't about commercial strategies and execution, but it must be said that these aspects are foundational to a strong culture. You can't create optimism about the future, a key element of employee engagement, without establishing the conditions for sustainability of the business itself. A highly engaged workforce will contribute greatly to the organization's ability to find and implement the right strategies and business models, especially as they are required to evolve over time. As CEO, you must ensure the right strategy and business model are in place to create the results needed to provide opportunities for people through the growth of the company.

When times get hard, it is not uncommon for all the attention to be paid to the criticality of responding to the challenges. That's not only normal, but it is also essential to effectively responding to acute threats to the business. As a metaphor, you wouldn't hold a party while the building burned. You'd put out the fire.

If the fire threat lasts a long time, the sustained emergency response mindset can start to erode the human connections. It takes personal, positive, supportive interactions—and a touch of humor—to maintain the kind of culture we are exploring together in this book, through difficult periods of the business. If I'm working long hours for months on end to help my company survive, but all my interactions with others are sterile, terse and transactional, I'm going to start feeling distant. I'm going to start questioning why I'm working so hard.

This is one of the hardest things about being a CEO in difficult times. Hard, that is, if you care about the people in your business and take personal responsibility for ensuring their livelihoods aren't threatened. If you aren't that kind of CEO, hard times are just a math problem—how many people do I have to cut to protect profitability as my revenue drops or my margins shrink? As I write this, we are seeing in real time how lofty cultural statements are being contradicted by the layoffs at Twitter, Alphabet, Amazon, Meta, Shopify and many others. Tens of thousands of people got their termination notice by text or email. "Don't be evil", indeed.

But if you do care, you must be conscious about how your behavior, and the behavior of all your leaders, communicates that care—and your confidence—even as you focus on taking effective, prompt action to protect the organization.

If you have a strong culture, and you're leading with care and a bias to act, economic shocks or major company-threatening events will create *increased* cohesion. During the three years of the pandemic, WD-40 Company conducted a special version of the engagement survey, to "check in" on how people were feeling and to ask them what advice or ideas they may have to respond to some of the challenges we faced. The engagement index rose from the pre-pandemic survey completed in January of 2020. We think this was in part because the tribe felt safe within the organization, as the world was chaotic around them. They felt safe for a reason: the company's business design and methods were built on economic and human sustainability, even in hard times. I'll address crucial elements of that design in the chapter on compensation.

Sound strategy, strong leadership in creating and sustaining business health are foundational, fully equal (not superior) to how you lead people, in creating a highly engaged organization.

WHAT IS YOUR PHILOSOPHY OF LEADERSHIP?

The next part of the culture "engine" you create relates to your personal views of the proper role of a leader in your organization. What do you expect leaders to do? What is the difference between a leader and an individual contributor?

Many companies do not consciously address this essential topic. Others do, but don't hold the same views of leadership behaviors that result in higher engagement. I have continually wondered why, with the clear opportunity that higher engagement creates, both qualitatively and quantitatively, more CEOs don't pursue the actions necessary to increase engagement. An article in the April 2023 Economist may have shed some light on the mystery.

The article, "Managing Expectations" appeared in the Schumpeter column. It talked about the curriculum found at one of the most prestigious leadership schools, the Graduate School of Business at Stanford University. The Harvard and Stanford business schools combined currently have about 1,300-1,500 students, with Harvard's enrollment twice that of Stanford. Harvard's two-year MBA program is about $147,000 for tuition. Stanford's is higher, at about $153,000. The grades required to qualify, along with the total costs of attendance including living expenses, mean that most of the people who graduate already have means, and are likely destined for significant leadership roles in corporations. For example, the current prime minister of the United Kingdom, Rishi Sunak, is a graduate of Stanford's business school. His career included a stint at Goldman Sachs and he was a partner at two hedge funds. Now he leads a country.

The Schumpeter article explored the emphases of the coursework at these "top" business schools. One of the most popular elective courses within the curricula at Stanford is "Paths to Power", a course that purports to lessen the odds of failure due to "insufficient sensitivity to, and skill in, coping with power dynamics". The instructor, Jeffrey Pfeffer, explains that the objective of the course is to ensure that "you never have to leave a position involuntarily". One of the methods of achieving this goal, as taught in the course, is to not groom a competent successor.

This type of preparation for leadership might explain some of the retardation in engagement within companies—famous and coveted schools which purport to educate future business leaders seem to be offering coursework that is antithetical to the type of leadership which does increase engagement.

There is also the distinct possibility that leaders just haven't consciously thought about how they lead, or what the role of leadership is supposed to contribute.

From my personal leadership experience, my observations of many others and my two-plus decades working with WD-40 Company, I have composed a definition of a leader's accountabilities that correlates to high engagement and high performance:

- A leader is accountable for whether others do or do not achieve the results needed.
- A leader is accountable for the quality of life that others experience while at work.
- A leader is accountable for teaching and mentoring others, ensuring they have developmental experiences which allow them the opportunity to grow in their chosen career.
- A leader is accountable for coaching others to advance in their capabilities.
- A leader is accountable for looking as far ahead as possible.
- A leader is accountable for making the decisions that cannot be delegated and must be made.

You can tell by my choice of words that I have a philosophy of leadership often referred to as "servant leadership". I sometimes think labeling such leadership behaviors as a "type" of leader could be a problem. If there is "servant" leadership, then there is "non-servant" leadership, indicating that both are valid options. I just think there's leadership, done well or not done well. But I'll use the term here to indicate the full set of descriptive behaviors we're talking about.

As I said before, when I met WD-40 Company and its leaders, I found instant alignment in the definition of what a leader should be. Garry Ridge demonstrated by his own behavior that he was a continual learner, and he felt the proper role of a leader is primarily to be a teacher. He instituted the use of the term "coach" to mean a person's immediate supervisor. A coach acts in service to those led, intent upon helping them succeed. Garry co-authored a book on this subject with Ken Blanchard, called "Helping People Win at Work: A Business Philosophy Called Don't Mark My Paper, Help Me Get an 'A'". Having learned the concept from Ken and his wife Margie during his coursework to earn a master's degree in Executive Leadership at the University of San Diego, he immediately felt resonance with the approach.

Servant leadership is not servile leadership. It is a leadership philosophy that says the leader is performing the needed role of guiding others and making decisions to ensure that the people for whom they are accountable have the best chance of success as possible, as individuals and as a group.

We've all heard the data that says the relationship between a person and their immediate manager is the single most influential reason why employees decide to leave a company—or decide to stay. I have seen the truth of this fact throughout my working life, for myself and for countless others.

How do you, as CEO, behave as the kind of leader people will follow? In other words, why should someone walk through a brick wall for you?

I've worked for leaders who inspired just this kind of commitment, engagement, and motivation. I would attempt ambitious achievements for them. It was a pleasure to be in their company. They made me feel respected, foremost. They demonstrated by their behavior and their words that I was needed and important to the success of the organization. And I respected them for what they knew, their skills and their own demonstration of commitment. I saw that they worked just as hard as everyone else did, including doing the mundane tasks that we all had to do. They filled the stapler and the printer ink when they ran out. They worked on the weekend when everyone else was asked to. They were aware of my breaking point and found ways to reduce pressure when it was important for my health. They fundamentally cared about me as a human being.

The "Great Resignation", "Quiet Quitting" and other catchy phrases have popped up in recent years, meant to capture a supposed new trend in employee attitudes. These patterns describe a situation that has been nothing if not perennial, rather than novel. Whenever crises occur for an organization, a country or the world, motivations are tested, and people can decide to make a change. Some of you may remember the Financial Crisis of 2008-2009, and the resulting Great Recession that took seven years to dig out of. Prior to that we had other global economic storms. Each such crisis tested leaders, and the commitments of the people in those organizations.

Just like those earlier calamities, during the stresses of the pandemic and the related supply chain earthquakes, organizations asked their people to walk through metaphorical brick walls that required every ounce of very real energy. The more engaged organizations, those with stronger relationships and the kind of leaders who do inspire willingness to do the brick battering, fared far better than others without those elements.

But even culturally strong, close-knit companies risk tattered threads if they forget that leadership must still earn followers in the same exact ways it has always been earned, since the time when workers escaped indentured servitude. Taking that commitment for granted is the first step in destroying it. The conscious leader, the servant leader, continually asks "Why would someone walk through a brick wall for me?" If the leader cannot articulate the reasons outlined here the answer is, "They wouldn't". And they really shouldn't.

As you examine whether you are such a leader who inspires others to achieve amazing things, ask yourself, "Why did I want to be a leader?" Your motivations to lead are transparent to everyone who works for you and with you, revealed by your actions. Even if you don't completely understand your own reasons to lead.

Some people, maybe a lot of people, don't consciously choose leadership in advance. They are invited to become a manager when they are excelling in their work. The pay and the title are attractive. So, they step into the job without truly understanding what it means. Over time, they may be happy they did accept the role, or they might find they don't really like the added accountability, the lack of direct control over the results they are responsible to achieve, the constant demands on their time, dealing with human relations issues, etc. Every leader should examine their motives to lead.

Here are the five reasons I've catalogued in my observations of human behavior, as to why a person pursues a leadership role and career:

1. Higher income
2. Desire to have more autonomy and control over decisions

3. A desire to help other people
4. Wanting to feel the elevation of status, prestige and advancement that comes with leadership positions
5. The job needs to be done by someone, and there's no one better volunteering

These various motivations to be a leader can be operating singly or in combination. Let's take a look at each.

Higher Income

It is true that to achieve the higher income levels in most career fields it is necessary to go up the leadership ladder. But that reason loses its appeal after a while because whatever greater compensation is achieved, if there is no other reason behind one's desire to advance in leadership roles, the work itself becomes less and less meaningful. And it is well-established that once the higher income is in effect, it takes less than a year before the money loses its behavioral reinforcement properties. We get used to the new level quickly. It becomes a "hygiene" factor in our motivation, as the psychologists phrase it: when the money is coming in, we are *not dissatisfied.* But we're not actually satisfied.

I once had a client who owned a real estate development company. His net worth at the time was about $200 million. He was in the process of building the biggest, most expensive home in Rancho Santa Fe, a community of San Diego County that is one of the wealthiest enclaves on the planet.

As I was coaching him, each time we met he would offer his reasons why he felt he was successful. I hadn't asked the question. He just felt compelled to tell me every time we met.

His reasons were all about his financial achievements. After months of working with him, at a coaching session, he said, "You know, the reason why I feel like I've succeeded is that I don't know anyone who has more money than I do, with whom I'd want to trade places." I asked him, "If you meet such a person, would you no longer feel successful?" He didn't have an answer.

There is no finish line for the motivation of money.

People who work for such a leader are not inspired to sacrifice, serve others, contribute as a team member, or think beyond the dollars. If they stay, they learn to be self-centered, concerned about how much of the pie they are getting and compete with everyone else within the organization.

Autonomy

The motivation of more autonomy and decision-making control is often found to be an illusion. Sure, a leader can make more decisions than an individual contributor, but not a lot more. And those decisions still need willing support from those led to have the decision turn into the expected results. The leader can't force someone's hands to move on a keyboard, turn a wheel, create a report, lift a package, make a phone call, etc. And as a CEO, you know that you are always "reporting" to someone else anyway, whether it's your customers, your shareholders, your board of directors, regulatory agencies…the list goes on.

Even if you are making a lot of the decisions, that will only limit the ability of your organization to grow beyond your personal capacity. I quote Garry Ridge a lot. A key realization of his, early in his tenure as CEO of WD-40 Company, was that "micro-management isn't scalable". So true.

Therefore, the motivation of full autonomy turns out to be a goal that is difficult if not impossible to achieve, if you are leading an organization of more than a few people.

Helping People

The motive to "help" people might sound like servant leadership, but it's not really aligned with that philosophy, if by "helping" you are creating co-dependency. The "helping" leader is someone who wants to feel of value to others, to be accepted and praised for their support. Employees who enjoy working for a "helping" leader experience less accountability for results and fall into the habit of learning how to need the help. It's similar to the over-protective parent who steps in to solve problems for their children, preventing the scraped knee or breaking up the tussle before their kids learn to do it themselves. The child learns to wait for the help and doesn't increase their ability to solve their own challenges. It's the same dynamic with the "helping" leader. This reality is another reason why I don't like the phrase, "Take care of your people". For one thing, they aren't "my" people. I don't own them. We are equal beings with different responsibilities. Taking care of them infers protecting them from harm and satisfying all their needs. That is a parental way of viewing the leader's role, which I'll talk about in the chapter on building a culture of accountable adults. This type of leadership does not create true engagement; it creates entitlement and learned helplessness.

Status

A leader who is attracted to "advancing" up the leadership ladder wants the feeling of status and prestige that can accompany the elevation. There are still a lot of organizations who actively appeal to that motivation. Executives are placed on a higher floor in the building. They get the coveted corner office, and the office is bigger than anyone else's. They get a parking spot that is convenient, while others must walk a quarter mile to the front door. They fly first class while other employees hunker in coach. People motivated by elevation of status can be heard to speak of being the leader with comments like, "The view is better if you're the lead dog on the sled".

If that is your motivation to lead, you will be communicating your disdain for people "lower" in the hierarchy simply by availing yourself of the trappings of capitalism's royalty. And you don't have to be the CEO to create a negative effect by this motivation's demonstration. Even a first-line supervisor can behave in a way that says, "I'm better than you are now. I have privileges you don't have."

The only people who will happily follow a status-driven leader are those who similarly want the same. If the organization is largely made up of such people, there is constant competition for recognition, access to senior leaders, the next promotion to the next better office, etc. There is no "we", just a bunch of "me-s". There are huge companies who still today follow this philosophy of leadership. They make a lot of money. I wouldn't want to work in any one of them. I think there are more people who don't want that kind of environment than there are who do.

Service

The motivation to rise into leadership because it needs to be done, and no one else is stepping up who is better able, is the most objective, selfless and enduringly rewarding reason to be a leader. I say this out of personal experience, and observation of thousands and thousands of people, across all kinds of companies and industries, over nearly 50 years of being a student of human behavior in the context of business. This motivation is the foundation of servant leadership, i.e., being of service to the entire organization by performing the role of a leader.

We're all human. All five motivations apply to all of us, particularly at varying times in our life, at least to some degree. But ask yourself, "Which one of these five motivations to lead is the *biggest* source of my desire to be a leader?" If you're not sure, you can ask the people you lead what they think your motivations are. They watch your behavior daily and are likely more capable of answering the question for you than you are. If they feel safe enough to be honest.

In the Leadership Lab of WD-40 Company, we openly explored these motivations together, allowing people to discover their own truth and examining the reasons to choose leadership. Leadership Lab was our experimental setting of leadership, inviting exploration, questioning and self-reflection. During my time as HR leader of the company we completed over 30,000 student-hours of leadership workshops, around the world. Why go through so much effort, you might ask?

Many years ago, in my early thirties, I was applying for a position at what was then Martin Marietta Aerospace

Corporation. The division near San Luis Obispo was hiring for an organizational development specialist. Brandishing my newly minted master's degree in organizational psychology and several years of experience, I applied.

I was interviewed by the hiring manager, who had a Ph.D. in psychology. He looked just like the stereotypical college professor, including the pipe and sport coat with patched elbows. His office was outfitted with a large blackboard on the wall. Chalk was still used in those days, rather than whiteboards and markers.

After some preliminary dialogue, the "professor" asked me a question: "Stan, which method of creating sound leadership results do you think is preferable? Do you focus on developing strong leaders capable of handling many scenarios, or do you provide leaders with strong guidelines and policies for them to follow, to address the scenarios they will encounter?"

I thought about it for a few moments, then responded: "I think you must focus on developing strong leaders who understand the principles and methods of leadership and can operate autonomously based on those enduring internal skills."

The professor asked why. I said that leaders who were independently capable of leading well would be more likely to respond effectively and quickly in the face of changing environmental dynamics. At that moment, I noticed for the first time that on his credenza were no less than a dozen Martin Marietta management policy and procedure manuals.

I didn't hear from him for months after the interview. During that time, I accepted a role at TRW. When the professor eventually called to offer me the job, I let him know that I had since found a position. I guessed that the management procedure for bringing on a new person in his department took three months.

But since that interview, I have periodically questioned my answer to the professor. I have examined the evidence in the field, so to speak, and I continue to conclude that my answer was correct. Much of my work since then has involved solving the challenge of how to develop good leaders. Most of the development must be achieved on the job under the guidance of an experienced leader who has trod the path. But educational efforts can provide principles and examples to better prepare the student leader for those on-the-job realities. For example, you take longer to achieve proficiency as a bass player if you don't learn the scales and chord progressions first before you're thrown on stage.

At HRG, we created leadership coursework that included numerous topics, focusing on the underlying principles of human behavior and leadership, not the least of which was how to lead in a manner that inspired willing followers. We had many clients who participated. When I joined WD-40 Company, I brought this leadership curriculum with me, which formed a core set of courses. Along with my talented colleagues at the company, we then expanded and improved that set of workshops. My fellow "faculty" contributed immeasurably to the content and quality of what became a cornerstone of internal leadership development. Today, Leadership Laboratory covers about 20 courses and is conducted both in person and virtually, around the world.

One of the most impactful and powerfully educational workshops we offered was completing the personal inquiry that resulted in your Leadership Point of View (LPOV). The LPOV arrived at WD-40 Company from our engagement with the Ken Blanchard Companies (now simply called Blanchard). Ken Blanchard and his organization approached leadership from the humanistic perspective, long before it became the current popular topic. Blanchard designed the LPOV to begin building leadership abilities through first examining one's own path of life. Through specific queries that are answered honestly and carefully, many people who complete an LPOV achieve self-understanding for the first time in their lives, on the topic of leadership. They identify the seminal experiences and the influential people who affected them, which collectively resulted in how they view leadership, what their values are, and what they may understand is their life's purpose.

The LPOV queries ask about who in your life was an impactful leader, a person who taught you something (good or bad). The LPOV asks what your values and purpose are, and how you arrived at them. The LPOV asks what you expect of others, and what they should expect from you. When I did it for the first time, it was a revelatory experience. While I knew what my values were, I had not put together the story of my journey in such a way as to fully understand where my values and views of leadership came from, and why they are important to me.

When you complete an LPOV, that's only part of the process. The next step is to get comfortable telling your story to other people. In our Leadership Lab workshops, people would compose their LPOV, then share it with one other person, serially. Then people would volunteer to address the entire group in the workshop. There were tears. There was laughter. And everyone, to a person, became closer to each other. Such shared vulnerability creates deep trust and a bond that endures.

As CEO, you must start with yourself. Do you know yourself well enough to describe your own motivations to lead? Do you know your own story? Can you articulate your leadership philosophy to others? And if others hear it, will it increase or decrease their desire to walk through a brick wall for you when you ask them to?

If you decide to adopt the philosophy of servant leadership for your organization, and you truly believe that a leader's primary role is that of a teacher, helping people succeed along the paths they have chosen, then you must be a student of leadership yourself, and teach it within your company.

It's my conclusion that every organization should invest in the growth of their leaders. No leader is beyond developing further. As they say, "To *know* is to stop learning." Leaders set the bar for the acceptable behavior in the organization. If you and your leaders are sending people to educational experiences so that they can grow and develop, but you are not stretching your own abilities, then why should they? If your senior leaders don't also demonstrate humility and a desire to learn, then it will be very difficult to achieve the kind of culture and performance that are possible if you all did. It is still true that one bad apple can spoil the barrel. *Every* leader is critical to building and maintaining the strong organizational culture you desire. If you are a CEO attending the Culture Forum, you've just demonstrated the behavior of continual learning that will likely be emulated by others in your organization.

Another reason to invest in leadership development is that effective succession preparation is accomplished first and foremost by developing the abilities of everyone already in the company. Succession is fulfilled by building the bench of capable people who are ready to step up when called. And it is my opinion that the most senior leaders in a company should primarily be drawn from people who have spent many years in the organization, earning their advancements through demonstrating the values and achieving strong results. Hiring leaders from other organizations can be successful, if the candidates are carefully and accurately evaluated, of course. But trusting relationships are more powerful in affecting leadership ability than expertise. It takes time to build those relationships, through a variety of experiential contexts.

When Leadership Laboratory was launched in 2012, it followed certain principles of adult learning that have resulted in many people acquiring leadership knowledge and skill (whether or not they pursued roles that were positions of formal leadership). These principles were consciously selected to reinforce the characteristics of the culture felt to be critical.

Here are the principles we employed in WD-40 Company's Leadership Laboratory:

- Everyone is invited because everyone leads in some way.
- Course participants are not segregated by "level" in the company. Everyone is in the same room, equal human beings who have varying responsibilities.

- Everyone has high potential and earn advancement according to their demonstrated abilities and contributions.
- Participation is voluntary.
- Learning requires the commission of well-intentioned, intelligent mistakes; these are welcomed as "learning moments", as we say at WD-40 Company.
- People are accountable for their own future; they must decide what they want and be willing to work towards achieving their objectives.
- Participation does not reduce performance expectations or goals.

The last two principles mean that when people engage in professional development activities, they are investing time and energy in themselves, while still achieving the contributions needed from their role. At WD-40 Company, as well as my other business adventures, we invested in people who were willing to invest in themselves. Think about that. It means that people earn their opportunities to learn. Too often, companies take a parental approach to learning and development programming. People are coaxed to participate. They are accommodated with relaxation of expectations. They are courted and cajoled. These actions give people the message that they are "owed" something and that their participation should be compensated in some way. That is exactly the wrong messaging and sets up an entitlement mentality. The opportunity to learn *is* the reward.

The other negative dynamic is requiring people to participate. When it's a mandate, the mindset of the participant is often one of resentment and skepticism that the time spent will be of any value. Such forced attendance ensures that much of the value of the learning simply bounces off the participants and creates a ready-made excuse as to why other goals aren't being achieved: "I had to sit through two days of workshops so I couldn't get the project done on time."

In the Leadership Lab we also explored the experiences of leadership that contribute to someone becoming the kind of leader that others will willingly follow. Here are some of the most important character-building experiences that are foundational to a leader's development:

- Rising to a position of leadership from that of a peer; making the adjustment in relationships
- Trusting others to perform when your own job security and performance results are a function of what other people do or don't do
- Owning the accountability for performance shortfalls when you aren't directly responsible for them. The leadership mantra: "There are lots of reasons. There are no excuses."
- Putting your own comfort and desires aside to provide the leadership that others need
- Sharing the pain and stress of difficult times along with those whom you lead (rather than asking them to work the weekend while you go golfing)
- Telling people the truth, with care and candor, about their demonstrated abilities and behaviors, even if they respond angrily, despondently, or not at all
- Demonstrating leadership qualities daily that inspire others to follow you
- Having to give someone corrective performance guidance

- Having to make the decision to separate someone from the organization
- Having to separate someone from the organization that you hired and/or promoted
- Admitting you made a big mistake to your own team, to your peers, to your own leader, without deflection or excuse

Each experience tests your character, your ability to be honest with yourself and others, your willingness to look in a mirror when things go wrong, and through a window when they go right. Each experience is the formative base of how you evolve further as a leader. My first mentor in the world of corporations, Louis Paglialonga, once told me, "Learning how to lead comes the same way as learning how to stand up for yourself—one bruise at a time."

As people completed the three levels of Leadership Lab coursework over a period of a few years, some of them expressed a desire to be teachers themselves, so our faculty expanded. As you may agree, the way you really learn a topic is to attempt to teach it to someone else. We reasoned that if we had tribe members learning and then teaching these subjects, they would more likely be highly competent in acting with those principles embedded in their behavior. They would also be getting leadership experience in the process. And finally, our growing internal "faculty" amplified our ability to provide educational experiences to many more tribe members. Some people designed whole new courses of specific professional topics, like Project Management and Financial Literacy. Many of our leadership roles were filled by graduates of the Leadership Lab.

We would routinely get feedback from senior leaders who joined workshops that included every type of role and level in the leadership progression. They said things like, "I learned more about this company in that set of workshops than I have in the last ten years", and "I learned from people who I wouldn't have predicted could teach me about leadership", and "Participating helped me form stronger relationships throughout the organization, beyond my direct reports".

For over twenty years, we also sent one to three people a year to a Master of Science program in executive leadership (MSEL) at the University of San Diego, the same program that Garry graduated from. This program was co-developed by Blanchard and USD, to include strong course content in leadership, along with the more customary graduate business school topics related to strategy, marketing, economics and the like. The pandemic has interrupted this program, but I would hope to see it return.

The applicants for these scholarships were invited from among the tribe, evaluated according to their position in their career development, their demonstration of sustained high performance and their aspirations for earning more accountable leadership roles. Almost all the graduates of the MSEL program accelerated their contributions in the years after completion, forming a very strong "bench" of candidates for new roles and succession needs. We additionally provided scholarships to applicants who earned the support for other graduate programs, including scientific and technical degrees. We also had educational reimbursement plans for everyone who wanted to invest in college level programs or specific, relevant conferences.

As CEO, you must participate in some way yourself, as an equal learner. Your demonstration of humility and the respect it shows to the others in the room will have an incredibly powerful and positive effect on how others trust you to lead them. And your senior executives must follow suit enthusiastically, not begrudgingly. Only leaders who are concerned about their perceived status will balk at joining an educational workshop along with non-executives. They may say, "I've had all that stuff already", which just means they don't think they have anything more to learn, from the course or the people in attendance. If they don't believe in personal continual improvement, why should the people they lead?

Your philosophy and strategy about leadership—what it means, how you teach it, how you demonstrate it—is an essential element in your journey to create the kind of culture that results in strong engagement. A key element of that strategy is your view of how to lead in a business, how things are decided.

My view is that businesses cannot be led like government. It is founded on the concept of private ownership and individual decision rights. With all its challenges and faults, capitalism in a democracy—which promotes entrepreneurialism, private ownership, fair competition, and the prohibition of fraud—has resulted in an incredible increase in the quality of life for billions of people. The United States is still the "land of opportunity" if you pay attention to the many, many success stories of people who either came here with nothing, or rose here from nothing, to create incredible lives for themselves and their families, and indeed many others who joined their commercial experiments. I would certainly count myself as a beneficiary.

My upbringing was in trailer parks, moving two or three times a year, part of the lower income tier with, shall we say, dysfunctional parents. I put myself through school, arriving at San Diego State University for my junior year after community college, with no job and $125 in my pocket. But I was blessed to be born in this country. I had only to apply myself to have the kind of life I'm so grateful to have lived thus far.

Business cannot be led entirely by consensus either. Consensus can be powerful and is a wonderful path to joint accountability. But sometimes the uncommon or unpopular idea is the best one. Insisting on 100% agreement results in the power shifting to the holdouts on any given decision. Sometimes you can't achieve consensus and a decision still needs to be made. That's a leader's responsibility.

As I've mentioned previously, I've seen the truth that business cannot be led by a raft of policy and procedure manuals. Change is constant. Only enduring, sound principles can serve to guide a leader's ability to choose the right path in complex, important, rapidly evolving situations. The policy manual hasn't been invented that could adapt at the speed of life.

As an example, at the outset of the COVID-19 pandemic in 2020, our global leadership formed an Issue Response Team. We had composed this emergency action process years before at WD-40 Company, which was triggered occasionally over time for periodic, unexpected, critical events. During the pandemic, we met weekly to address the new information, identify proper actions and communicate decisions globally. Early in the crisis I was often contacted by other companies asking what policies we were composing to respond. I told each of them that we were focusing on applying our values and our responsibility to lead week by week, because conditions were changing continually. By the time a set of policies might be written to address this week's reality, reality changed.

During my tenure at the company, I helped us move away from long lists of HR policies when principles and practices were more sustainably effective to address changing conditions. Sound principles in the hands of individually capable leaders created amplified, faster, and more effective action. Local leaders in each country translated those principles and practices into forms that were compliant with their local regulations and adapted to their local conditions.

You can engage with qualified and capable firms who offer educational programs to develop strong leaders. At WD-40 Company, we partnered with trusted firms as well, such as the Blanchard organization, and we invited guest speakers to our leadership meetings to add educational opportunity whenever our leaders convened for business purposes. But our internally created leadership development programs were essential to growing leadership ability that specifically matched our business, our culture, and our values. Our growing internal faculty of educational facilitators provided leadership experience for people who might not otherwise get that opportunity. I would suggest that you need to do both internal program development as well as employ external resources.

Be careful who you invite to influence your people, however. Not all leadership development programs are equal. Leadership programs delivered by people whose only work experience is delivering leadership programs will result in a lot of theory, but little practical experience to validate those theories. Academicians are highly knowledgeable about the content that academics create in their studies, but few have bet their own mortgage on those ideas. The people who have the best qualifications to teach leadership are the people who have themselves had significant leadership experience in a context relevant to your company. They must have some scars from their own development as a leader. They must have bet the time of their lives and their own income on their philosophies.

To summarize, my experience tells me that there is no substitute for having good leaders in your company, starting with yourself. Teaching people how to lead in the manner that you have defined and expect, aligned with your organizational values, creating a relationship of trust and respect between leaders and those led, is foundational to achieving the culture of high engagement and achieving your business objectives.

THE TRIBE

Garry introduced the cultural concept of the "tribe" to WD-40 Company early in his tenure as CEO. Having studied the history of the aboriginal people of Australia, his home country, he realized that the attributes of a tribe were descriptive of the kind of organization he wanted to live and work in.

A tribe is not as insular as a family but is much more than a team. A tribe is the collection of people that you will help to feed and defend. Tribes celebrate together and have strong traditions that create enduring bonds. Tribal elders have a duty to teach the coming generations the knowledge and wisdom that will help them succeed. Tribes are comprised of courageous defenders. Each tribe member has specialized skills to contribute to the welfare of all. Tribes have common values and principles of life. Tribes create a strong sense of belonging.

By using this term and defining it consciously, a common language was created, which represented reminders of our desired quality of interactions and increased the chances that we would adhere to the cultural principles, our values, and our purpose. This was most evident when we assembled. And those group events were intentionally designed. Whenever people gathered, there was always a component of education. There was always an opportunity for celebration.

The tribal "feel" and the strength of relationships created caused people to be personally concerned about each other's welfare. When someone was experiencing a personal crisis, people reached out to help. One year, a colleague of mine in HR was counseling an employee whose two-year-old child had been diagnosed with brain cancer. The amount of leave the mother required was far in excess of the time available to her through our benefits and vacation time programs. My colleague took initiative and did extensive research about the possibility of creating a voluntary leave donation plan, exhaustively analyzed the regulatory framework required and proposed a plan. We implemented it.

When the call went out by email one morning at 8:00 a.m. for volunteers to donate some of their vacation time to the employee whose child was facing a life-threatening illness, the full amount of needed time was satisfied by 8:02 a.m.

How you design your group events is another critical element of culture creation. Whenever people gather, it is an opportunity to form and reinforce interpersonal connections. And always leave room in the agenda for unstructured time. This is where people can have those unscripted, spontaneous interactions that create positive lasting memories. Thanks to open slots on the agenda, I've had many.

One year at a meeting in the U.K. in the Cotswalds, I was attending the planning sessions for the European business. We had scheduled free time one evening. I will never forget the two hours I spent in the ancient castle's pub, talking about the history of American blues and rock with the director of the distributor markets, an expert on the subject even though he was a Brit. Every time I saw him at future meetings, we had a special connection.

On a trip to Shanghai, the local HR leader invited me and my colleague visiting from the U.S. to join her on an excursion to the Yellow Mountains for the special experience of watching sunrise from one of the peaks. These geologic formations are unlike any mountain you have ever seen elsewhere. They are essentially pillars jutting skyward thousands of feet, out of the misty fog at their bases, ablaze when the sun rises over the horizon. Shirley didn't have to spend her weekend with us. She didn't have to take the time to arrange our travel. We had an incredible experience, thanks to her thoughtfulness.

When people go out of their way to make a human connection with each other, to create experiences of life together, that is the surest sign that your culture is self-sustaining. Because everyone is creating the belonging. It's not just a mantra repeated unthinkingly, or superficial behavior designed to deflect scrutiny in front of leaders. These types of experience happened to all of us all the time, over multiple events, over multiple years.

Whenever a large gathering of tribe members was called, it was usually a combination of business planning, education, and celebration. We would include service awards at such meetings, for example. The format of the service awards was not complex or expensive. The tenure pins were modest.

The leader whose tribe members were receiving an award, comprised of five-year increments of tenure, would stand before the entire crowd with the recipient next to them. Without notes, the leader would recount the history of the tribe member, their accomplishments, their unique talents. The leader would always include some warm story that revealed the humanity of the tribe member. And of course, embarrassing, fun moments from the past were relived. There was always laughter, and often tears.

At gatherings of the tribe, the casual observer watching the interactions would not likely be able to identify any hierarchy. Everybody engaged with everybody else, no matter their role or position in the leadership structure. Garry would be seen talking with the customer service specialist just as likely as the managing director of Europe, Middle-east, Africa and India. When people would ask me about the type of culture we have at WD-40 Company, I would respond, "We take our work very seriously, not ourselves." People didn't flaunt their importance, flash their titles, or evaluate which group they should be seen with in order to appear important.

Referring to leaders as a "coach" rather than "manager" also exemplifies the tribal role of the elder, that of a teacher, as discussed in the earlier chapter on leadership philosophy. As people use that term, it reinforces the behavioral repertoire that accompanies the word. Simply by using "coach", the behaviors of leaders and those led changed. The relationship becomes more mutually engaging, because it's about the success of the tribe member, not about catching someone doing something wrong or exerting authority over another person.

You can decide what type of cultural terminology to employ, specific to your objectives and your own style. The words you choose, and the meaning they convey, are powerful, however. Choose wisely. Thought creates language, but language also creates thought. This has been proven by neuroscientific study. Choose your culture consciously and choose how you communicate within your organization with deep intention. Behaviors you exhibit, and that you desire, will be reinforced. The common language will be glue, binding people together in a shared experience of the organization.

A note about cultural misappropriation and the use of the word "tribe". I fully understand that "first peoples" in America and many other places were displaced (to put it clinically) by colonialists from other parts of the world. Not a proud history, but a true one. I do not want my behavior to convey in any way that I think it was okay to "displace" a huge mass of humanity simply because of want and ability. I understand the visceral negative reaction that, say, a Hopi tribe member might have, hearing me explain that my company was a tribe.

The intent of using the word "tribe" is to honor the jewels of relationship that exist within a tribe, and to hopefully emulate them. It is to honor that part of all humanity's legacy, a very large part of us, which was created over hundreds of thousands of years of our ancestors living in hunter-gatherer tribes. By demonstrating the qualities of a tribe, I feel I am demonstrating respect for "first peoples" everywhere they existed.

CRITICAL MASS

As CEO, you are the first and most important, essential component in building your culture engine. But you also need other people in your company who want to go in the same direction as you do, especially other leaders. There is a certain proportion of such people that must be achieved to ensure progress is made and cultural achievements sustained.

It's not possible to expect that everyone will be fully devoted to the principles of high engagement or behaving congruently with them all the time. Even you. I haven't met a saint yet, especially when looking in the mirror. But if your intentions are true and you have enough commitment from others, you will help each other through the lapses. You will have critical mass to achieve "ignition" and the momentum to carry your culture through the inevitable challenges to its existence over the years to come.

Your senior leaders, those who report directly to you, must be *completely* aligned with the cultural objectives. They must demonstrate commitment to the values by how they behave. They must be truly inspired by the purpose. They must agree on the leadership philosophy, although they can still be learning and developing—it's about progress, not perfection, and demonstrating transparent acknowledgement of what they have yet to learn, in how to apply the principles presented here. When someone might falter on the path, it should be expected that others will be brave enough to say so. If you invite periodic assessment of your own congruent behaviors, it will give others courage to do the same.

If you don't have complete alignment from your direct reports, it's like driving a car with one flat tire. You can still drive, but you damage the vehicle, and you don't go very fast along your course.

Assuming you have that alignment amongst your senior leadership team, the next question is, who else is not aligned? Each level of leadership from first line through middle management is going to either represent strong brickwork or sand, in the structure of your culture. Each relationship between a leader and those led is an opportunity to reinforce the culture you are creating—or erode it.

In my experience, the necessary critical mass of leadership alignment among those who report into senior leaders is about 60%, to make good progress. If you have that ratio of committed leaders in those roles, it will usually bring along those who are undecided or unsure of the cultural objectives and leadership philosophy. It won't ensure conversion of leaders who actually object to your cultural journey, however. With at least 60% enthusiastically committed, and 30% willing to go along and give the cultural journey the benefit of the doubt (or at least not act in contradiction to your values, purpose, and leadership philosophy), the remaining 10% will have much less of a negative influence. You'll still need to invite them, teach them, and counsel them. They may evolve. If they don't, you must decide whether they should continue in the organization.

Such decisions are not easy, and you must engage with these leaders with the same intent to help them succeed as anyone else. One of the premises of servant leadership coaching is that you don't give up on someone before you make a strong effort to truly help them grow. I have seen people respond well to what I will call "cultural coaching", to help them see the value of the behaviors that reinforce engagement and assist them in learning those behaviors, within their unique style and personality. People don't have to be robots in how they behave, to align with an engagement-reinforcing culture. I've had leaders who inspired me and treated me with deep respect but did so in dramatically different ways.

Harder is the case when a culturally misaligned leader has other attributes that are important to the company and may be in short supply in the talent market. Back to values: sometimes they cost you to keep them. If you really want to create a values-driven, purposeful organization where people want to be for a long time, you may have to separate someone who is acting in contradiction to those objectives, even if their absence causes short-term pain for the organization.

We certainly had such occasions at WD-40 Company, and I've experienced it personally in the businesses I've founded and/ or led. Sometimes people did change their minds and decided to work towards acting differently. However, not infrequently when the issues were directly addressed, the individuals chose to take their life journey somewhere else voluntarily. In each case where this was necessary, the act of separating a leader, or when they decided to leave, resulted in both a sense of relief by others around them and increased confidence in the culture. People stepped up to help cover the short-term gaps, if needed.

Of course, individual contributors also need to behave according to the values and in alignment with the purpose of the company. But leaders have amplified impact on the organization. And the more accountability of the role, the higher the volume of that amplification.

If you're not sure where your leaders are in their thinking about the topic of culture, of values, of purpose, the first step is to find out. Taking them along the journey with you, inviting them to explore the topics and examining their own beliefs is a good way to start. This is why our Culture Forum requires an organization's CEO to attend, but encourages CEOs to bring others with them, so that the CEO leads by example and invites others to join. Instructing people to follow you won't change minds, but your commitment and an earnest invitation to join you in exploring this path will more likely gain willing participants.

PERFORMANCE TRACKING AND REPORTING

This topic is perennially debated and there has been an ongoing effort to find the perfect methodology, the right forms and more recently, the best online application. While I do recommend a particular process, even what I might suggest is less important than the quality of the relationship between the leader, i.e., the "coach", and the person who relies on that coaching. The absolute best form to use for performance evaluation tracking and feedback is a blank sheet of paper, used to capture the rich and frequent dialogue that has occurred between a person and their immediate, capable, caring leader.

There is a plethora of online performance tracking tools that propose to make the process more efficient and timely. But you can't have a personal, trusting relationship with a software tool. Humans must interact with each other in three dimensions to form strong bonds, increase understanding and establish mutual appreciation. All senses must be in play to fully experience another person. It's best to interact in person as much as possible, but at least two dimensions in real time are required, *after* a strong relationship is built in three.

At WD-40 Company, we did use a form. It contained sections that were intended to remind people of the important elements of "helping people win at work". The functional requirements and goals of the role were outlined, at the outset of the performance period (fiscal year), which could include goals that had multi-year timelines. The tribe member is accountable for tracking their own performance, recording progress, and evaluating their own level of contribution. The coach is accountable for ensuring meaningful dialogue happened at least once a quarter, when the discussion was about reviewing results honestly with the intention to guide the person to achieve objectives, performance metrics and career aspirations. The coach is accountable for factual and direct input about the person's level of ability and what may need to improve. The coach is also accountable to ensure that earned recognition is provided, to celebrate successes. The tribe member is accountable for their own career aspirations, investing in their own growth and making progress in developmental areas.

Included in the performance dialogue and captured in the document that recorded progress and discussions, are the values of the company. Each quarter, the tribe member is asked to describe behavioral examples of how they actually "lived" the values. The coach is also responsible for making such observations and sharing those with the tribe member.

The coach is accountable for the final content and evaluative statements. There is seldom much disagreement because the dialogue has been ongoing and candid throughout the performance period. Sometimes a disconnect does occur, even in a highly engaged culture. When there is such disagreement, it is usually because expectations were not truly clear, or honest dialogue didn't happen soon enough when corrective input was appropriate and needed, or when a person is harder on themselves than they should be and didn't hear enough positive feedback from their coach to correct their misconception.

The approach we took at WD-40 Company greatly reduced administrative work by the coaches, since everyone had just one performance document to track and complete. It also puts the tribe member in charge of their own performance tracking, as a trusted, accountable adult. This mindset increases engagement. I'll discuss additional ways of increasing the odds of people behaving as accountable adults in a later chapter.

At least annually, the coach and the tribe member would discuss the tribe member's aspirations for advancement in their career, or their desire to learn new skills, to get involved in different functional areas, to grow and learn. A plan would be composed at those meetings, with action items and follow-up to occur at each quarterly dialogue or as needed additionally.

At the end of the fiscal period, the final quarter's dialogue would be captured in the document. The tribe member and the coach would add their open-ended comments for posterity. The tribe member, the coach, and the coach's coach would all sign it, because both the immediate coach and their coach had accountability for ensuring the tribe member had the support and guidance needed to "win" at work. Signing the document is authorship of that accountability.

On that note, at WD-40 Company there was a "two-coach" methodology of leading people. Both the person's immediate coach, and also the coach's coach, are required to approve all employment-related actions: hiring, performance evaluations, compensation changes, role changes and the occasional need to counsel or separate someone. This two-coach principle ensures that such important decisions were done after appropriate consideration and thoughtfulness. Also, the person's second coach is openly available to interact with, to schedule time with for any reason. I encouraged my direct reports to get on Garry's calendar or take advantage of opportunities to interact with him. He is a great coach. They should have the chance to learn from him. And he should have the chance to get to know them better, particularly since he would need to make decisions, along with me, about their roles and their livelihoods.

A key point to remember is that the process and the paper (or even the online tool) are secondary to deep, informed, authentic, frequent, and effective interactions between a leader and those led. Entrusting each person to measure their own progress and performance increases the likelihood that they will actually achieve the performance they've committed to, and they will feel more control over their own work. Such a sense of autonomy is directly related to higher engagement.

ORGANIZATIONAL DESIGN TO INCREASE ENGAGEMENT

Your business strategy, determined by your values and purpose, translates into goals and metrics of success. The functional needs of your company to produce those results determine the form of how you organize work. "Form follows function" is a phrase espoused by architect Louis H. Sullivan in his 1896 essay "The Tall Office Building Artistically Considered", and principally followed by designers and engineers throughout subsequent history. It's the same for the "machinery" of your company.

Designing your company's functional structure includes what activities need to occur, how various functions will interact, how work gets done, etc. Creating an efficient and effective functional design for your organization is important to converting revenue into profit. It's also important to increasing engagement, because a clunky operational design of functions will frustrate people and make it harder for them to succeed.

Most people want to get work done well and as efficiently as possible. Few people like wasted time and energy. It can be highly demotivating when a person is asked to accomplish great things with poor tools, ill-designed processes, unclear or poorly defined accountabilities, insufficient budget, etc. If you want to positively affect engagement, make sure people have what they need to get the work done, and find ways to remove the speed bumps and detours along their journey.

Organizational design, the resulting job design, and the creation of career progressions within a functional field are ongoing challenges for any company. These elements require thoughtful attention so that the "engine" of the business is built in as durable a manner as possible, with clear pathways for personal advancement that match the needs of the company, now and into the future. Logical functional structure with clarity of roles and responsibility are important to people feeling engaged. Without it, people can lose respect for their leaders, even feeling like no one cares about how the poor systems create work and add time to their long workday.

Anticipating future needs that impact the organizational design can help you create career pathways that will be stable and useful in future decisions about hiring, advancement and compensation. Career pathways also provide your people with a view of what they could achieve over time if growth is successful. "Growth equals opportunity" is the mantra we followed at WD-40 Company.

An example was the evolution of the R&D function. In 2012, we began the process of translating long-term (7-10 year) growth objectives and strategies into the likely functional needs of R&D that would be required to support that growth. We identified the need to establish regional scientific capabilities, both internally and contracted, to support the product development demands due to market opportunities, regulatory evolution specific to various countries and our chosen strategies for growth within those markets.

The organizational design process we followed is a systems approach that formally assesses functional needs, capacity requirements now and in the future by type of activity and the specific performance metrics appropriate to track. The study resulted in the identification of future R&D roles that would become important to fill as we achieved various growth and product innovation milestones. So, we designed a career progression for R&D, including both individual contributor and leadership positions that represented the functional needs anticipated, established their market value and salary ranges, and advertised their existence through our compensation transparency method (more on this topic in a later chapter).

Many of those roles remained unfilled for years. Then one day, a growth stage was achieved, and the need arose to fill positions. The work had already been done, so there was no lag time between identifying the need and taking action to promote or hire someone into the role that became important to the business. Completing the architecture of your organization as it will look in the future is a key tool in accelerating your ability to grow.

A key element in organizational design that is sometimes overlooked, or not given sufficient conscious attention, is the topic of decision rights. One of the most debilitating causes of organizational dysfunction is the condition of vague authority.

Unclear authority can exist in any role, but it is often found in organizational design structures that follow a "matrix" approach. A matrix structure typically collects enabling functions along one axis, whose services are delivered to commercial functions which have the accountability for revenue and profit. Another type of matrix structure is when there may be a role which has deeper expertise and the time to devote to specific functional projects, but which has no direct authority over the people partially performing that function within a business unit, division, or company. Matrix structures create "dotted line" reporting relationships, and they can be very confusing without explicit clarity of who does what and who has accountability for specific types of decisions.

At WD-40 Company, when a functional decision arose and it wasn't clear which role had the right and responsibility to make the call, we would routinely start the exploration of solutions with the question, "Who's decision is it?" As soon as decision rights were established, then we all knew our part to play in finding and implementing any given solution, performing a function, etc.

We also composed decision trees for issues that we could anticipate might come up without much warning. This was our Issue Response Plan, mentioned previously. Whenever such an event occurred, like the onset of the COVID-19 pandemic, we pulled out our plan and started down the path, knowing in advance who would be making the decisions, and our part to play in evaluating options, offering ideas, and eventually supporting whatever decision was made by the person who had the responsibility to call it.

Expecting people to "find a way" to collaborate, agree on actions and make decisions, simply because they "ought to be able to come to consensus", will only produce positive results occasionally, or when the stakes are not too high. If you want to prevent stasis in your business and encourage effective and efficient action by capable leaders, take the time to be explicit about "Whose decision is it?" Build the answers into the role descriptions, advertise it at the outset of an initiative or program, reinforce and clarify decision rights if confusion appears to arise. It's also important to say whose decision it *isn't*.

Delegating the right to decide is also a key method of developing leaders to be ever-more capable of making good decisions. You don't get good at decision-making unless you have a lot of opportunities to make increasingly impactful decisions, learning from your successes and your mistakes, or "learning moments".

Conscious attention to authority and decision rights will be another metaphorical shot of WD-40® Multi-Use Product to your engagement engine.

WHO YOU HIRE DETERMINES YOUR CULTURE

Our course on effective hiring methods at HRG was called, "Hiring Your Future". A company, or any organization, is nothing except the sum of its people, how they behave, how they do or don't work together in alignment, how they apply the capabilities they possess and how they demonstrate their character.

That's why, at WD-40 Company, we said "It's all about the people". This does not mean that leaders strive to satisfy every person's request or need. It means that the human factor is the most important determinant of whether your organization is a positive, rewarding place to be, where people are pulling on the same rope in the same direction as a team, accomplishing great things and having fun while they do it.

Of all the actions that you can take to positively affect your ability to create such an organization, deciding who to invite to join you is the largest contributor. Selecting the right people is probably the hardest business challenge there is, in my opinion. Even with the most thorough and effective methods, which are not easy to design or implement, hiring and promotion mistakes are inevitable. Humans are just too complex, and the variables are so many that predicting a successful match is a matter of probability. You can raise those chances, however, to a pretty high level.

Success in this effort begins with a clear definition of the qualities and characteristics of the "right" people, i.e., the definition of someone who "fits". If you don't have the right recipe to begin with, you really have little chance of ensuring a good choice.

The categories we used to determine "fit" at WD-40 Company included:

- **Competency** to perform the functions and achieve the objectives of the specific role: knowledge, skills, abilities derived from education and experiences likely necessary to achieve those competencies
- **Character** that is in alignment with the values of the organization
- **Aptitude** to learn and grow throughout their career, with the attitude of the curious, lifelong learner
- **Motivation** to fulfill the needed contributions of the role, with a sense of purpose and meaning in contributing to something larger than themselves
- **Team-orientation**, i.e., preferring to succeed as part of a collective effort, rather than working alone

None of these should be new to you, and likely would be on your list already. But what may need your attention is your method of determining a candidate's match to the criteria you have established.

There are a lot of tempting advertisements for short-cuts to finding the right people. Personality tests, "strengths" tests and other self-report "inventories" are numerous and loud in their claims of accuracy.

To date, I have found no such self-report survey or assessment that has criterion validity to any level that would make me confident I could rely on it to influence selection or promotion decisions. The purveyors of such tools will of course state that their assessments are not intended to be used to make hiring or promotion decisions, because they know they can't support such uses based on the data and they don't want a lawsuit. But they go on to describe how to "augment" hiring and promotion decisions using the tool. My view is that if it's not a criterion valid tool which can prove to be highly predictive of job performance, there's no evidence either that it can be any "augmentation" to the evaluation process.

"Criterion validity" means that the assessment tool has indeed been shown to predict job performance. This type of validity requires that the studies establishing criterion validity must demonstrate that they can predict both success *and* failure in a role, based on the results of the self-report test. There are few such tools which have criterion-validity that would pass peer review by psychometricians; however, none of these result in more than a small amount of prediction of variability on the performance scale used, at a level of statistical significance. And those tests are relevant to only a confined set of organizational or job criteria within specific industries where the studies were done.

Most psychometric tests offered to businesses claim only construct validity. This means that a model of behavior is created and then, based on self-report, the subject's position within that model is evaluated. The validity established is about the repeatability and reliability of results by the subject, and groups of subjects, in accordance with the model construct. This type of validity is self-referential and does not relate to objective behavioral results in any specific job. Myers-Briggs, DISC, Strengths Finder, I-OPT and many others are examples. You won't likely find any of these tests cited in peer-reviewed scientific literature. I have seen such tools be useful in the process of people learning how to be introspective and to examine their own thoughts, their own behaviors. But they are a start, not a finish. And they can offer the illusion of understanding using a temptingly simple tool, cutting short the rest of the journey of self-discovery.

A third type of proof is content validity. This means that the content of the evaluation method is directly related to the behavioral characteristics that have been proven to correlate to competencies and expected results of performing a given role, as evidenced by incumbents who are succeeding. This last method is not only more likely to be an accurate means of assessing a candidate, but also less expensive to apply and eminently pragmatic.

I have focused on the use of content-valid methods because 1) construct validity does not correlate to job performance, and 2) criterion validity is very difficult to establish with standardized self-report tests, and the few which do provide statistically significant results do not predict more than a small amount of performance variance. Both methods can be costly to administer, with very little juice resulting from the squeeze. Finally, 3) content-valid methods can be employed by existing professionals in your business with zero added costs, requiring only diligence in applying the thinking process.

To establish content validity, you start with a clearly defined set of behavioral criteria that you have internally validated as necessary, with evidence of those capabilities found in people who are performing the role well. If you don't have anyone in such a role within the organization yet, you can look to other organizations who do, to find the right set of behavioral capabilities.

Developed in the early 1980s, this method was called "core query". A query is any invitation for a person to behaviorally demonstrate the knowledge, skills, abilities, and characteristics which are correlated to success in a role. It's a type of behavioral interviewing. After the inception of core query methods, other behavioral interviewing methods proliferated, but tended to stray from the specifics of a given role and were broadened to include general behavioral traits of a variety of sorts, which may or may not apply to every role. I prefer the more specific approach and have found that when it's used diligently and consistently, it can increase predictive success to 80% or more.

The role definition is the place to start (commonly referred to as the job description). Without it, you cannot take the follow-on steps of identifying the ingredients required to be successful. I've seen many leaders avoid this step or use short-cuts like getting job descriptions from someone else's company or from a library of descriptions in a compensation survey. Those may or may not be applicable. If the hiring leader doesn't know the role well enough to compose it from scratch, how can they evaluate whether the borrowed job description is correct? Experienced leaders, which means leaders who have made hiring mistakes, soon come to the conclusion that they have to be rigorous in defining the role and defining the qualities, competencies and characteristics required to succeed.

Here are the major elements of a job description:

1. **Purpose**
   a. Why does this role exist at all? Why can't we do without this role?
   b. With a capable person in the role, what will have been accomplished in six months? A year? Three years?
2. **Essential Functions**
   a. What are the ongoing measurable activities and the expected results of this role, which would fulfill its purpose?
   b. What are the priorities of functions, from most important to least? Or are they all equal priority?
3. **What are the competencies a person would have to possess to be able to fully accomplish the expected results?**
   a. What is the specific knowledge needed to perform the role?
   b. What are the specific skills and abilities needed?
   c. What types of problems is this role expected to be able to solve independently? Which problems must be solved in concert with others?
4. **What are the accountabilities of this role?**
   a. What decisions does this role make alone? Which are shared, and with what other roles?
   b. What outcomes are uniquely expected from this role? What outcomes are shared, and with what other roles?

    c. What accountabilities for leading others does this role have, either directly or indirectly? What, if any, are the roles and number of people for whom this role is responsible?

    d. What is the magnitude of the expected outcomes, in terms of impact on the overall business?

    e. What is the time frame of impact that this role has? A week? A month? A year? Multiple years?

With careful and well-considered construction of the information above, now you are beginning to have the recipe for a successful hire. You have a clear idea of why you even need the position to be filled. You also have created a tool with which to compare to labor market trends of value for those competencies, which I will address in the chapter on compensation. You additionally have a great foundation for composing development plans to help people prepare for the role or improve within it. I can't stress enough how important this foundational work is to so many aspects of building the engagement "engine", starting with hiring the right people.

Now you're ready to design your candidate evaluation tools. Competency core queries should be composed so that they get to the heart of the subject and are constructed in such a way that the respondent cannot fudge their way through it with plausible but imprecise or misleading responses.

For example, if you are interviewing CFO candidates for a public company, which requires knowledge of disclosures required by the Securities and Exchange Commission, you could ask the following questions: "Are you familiar with SEC disclosure reporting?" If they say, "yes", you could then ask: "What are the types of disclosures which would require the submittal of SEC Form S-4? When would you need to submit Form S-5 instead?"

Asked in person, this question cannot be fluffed. The candidate either knows it or they don't. Such knowledge-based queries are relatively easy to compose and extremely useful in determining if someone truly has learned the role. Most interviewers of "senior" role candidates can feel embarrassed to ask someone a knowledge question because they don't want to "insult" the candidate, who may have decades of experience as a financial professional and executive. I can't tell you how often I've found such candidates incapable of answering the knowledge-based questions that their resume would indicate they should know as well as their own name.

Knowledge competencies are therefore straightforward to assess but take some thought. For example, if you are hiring a manufacturing engineer, you would want the incumbent to be able to know how to measure production factors that affect quality, quantity rates and costs. Usually that need involves understanding of statistical process control and how to apply inferential analytics to identifying causes of variance across production metrics.

You could ask candidates a question such as, "Have you applied statistical process control in a Six Sigma format to improve quality and production rates at the same time?"

"Yes, many times" they reply. This answer might give you confidence in their abilities, but it shouldn't. How many is "many"? And saying "yes" doesn't demonstrate that they can actually do the work.

A better question might be, "In an automated aerosol filling line, running at the rate of 500 finished cans per minute, what are the critical metrics you would assess to determine control levels required to achieve less than 10 rejections per hour?" And a follow up question could be, "When would you apply descriptive statistical analysis and when would you apply inferential statistical analyses to determine the range of control achieved in such a production line? What would you need to find out before selecting the right analytical tools?"

You could also hand them a set of reports on production, including statistical analyses that were completed, and ask them to interpret what they see in the reports.

Such queries greatly reduce the level of misunderstanding about someone's true abilities, take much less time to get to the answer of whether they match the role or not, and provide direct evidence of capabilities that cannot be derived from just noting their education and purported years of experience.

Another query methodology is to give the candidates an opportunity to demonstrate their abilities live. At WD-40 Company, when we were interviewing for candidates to fill the role of Director of Corporate Communications and Investor Relations, we asked finalist candidates to take our last few annual reports and present a shareholder briefing as if they were on a "road show" visiting the institutional investors who might consider acquiring our stock in the future. The interview panel acted as the potential shareholder audience. The person who knocked that demonstration out of the park became our new Director and has since earned promotion to Vice President. She's phenomenal.

But you're not done yet.

Along with the competencies, you still must measure character, aptitude, motivation and team-orientation.

How do you do that? The simple answer is that you provide candidates the opportunity to demonstrate by their behavior whether they can fulfill the functional accountabilities. And then you watch for character clues along the way, as to *how* they behave, their demonstrated authenticity, whether their words match their actions, whether they try to bluff their responses, and how they interact with the variety of people who encounter them during their candidacy.

Behavioral evidence trumps everything else. Good answers to your questions may be necessary, but they are insufficient to prove the match is good.

For example, you could ask an ethics or values question, like, "How do you feel your personal values align with ours?" The response could be fantastic: "I feel your company values could have been written by me. They are perfectly aligned with the kind of person I intend to be. Your second value of showing respect for all, for example, is nearly identical to an essay I wrote at age 12, for my class at Sunday school. Demonstrating respect for everyone is a foundation of my life. I still have that essay on my office wall to remind me of the character I'd like to exhibit daily."

As you escorted this wonderful candidate to the lobby and waved goodbye, you noticed that a colleague was scowling. You asked what was wrong. Your colleague says, "That jerk cut me off as I was entering the parking lot this morning. He looked right at me. Didn't apologize either when I walked by him as he waited in the lobby."

Often candidates will turn on the charm when they think they are in the presence of somebody who has influence over the hiring decision, and then behave naturally with others who they don't think have that influence. Getting behavioral observation feedback from everyone with whom a candidate comes into contact is important, whether or not they were part of the interview process formally. Especially if they weren't.

The discussions about compensation are another place to watch for character. If you ask early about what someone is hoping to earn and you've described the likely range offered in the role, how they respond and maintain a congruent response throughout the process reveals their approach to being candid and consistent about important subjects that affect people personally.

I've always recommended that you make an offer that is highest and best, according to the candidate's abilities to contribute to the role and the company's ability to afford it. You tell people this early in the exploration: "Should we make you an offer, it will be the absolute best we can do, within our labor market assessment for the role, and in alignment with our internal equity related to others in similar positions. We don't try to bargain with prospective new colleagues." You then ask for their honest range of preferred compensation and ensure that they know you will rely on their response in your deliberations. You tell them accurately what the compensation range is for the role. This sets up a dynamic of candor and trust-testing that can prevent surprises for both you and the candidate when you do offer the job. It also provides the chance to observe character in the candidate if you get to the offer stage. The offer process is therefore part of the candidate evaluation.

For example, if the compensation established and the candidate's stated desires are aligned throughout the interactions, but at the time of offer you start to hear new demands that push the boundaries of what you can consider, it's telling. This is how the person will approach such topics in the future, whether it's negotiating contracts with vendors or making agreements with other colleagues on how to complete projects or tasks. They will wait until they think they have leverage and then apply it for personal gain, at the expense of their integrity.

Aptitude can also be measured by behaviors. Of course, you can ask what examples the candidates might offer to demonstrate their aptitude for self-development, learning new things and succeeding in new types of responsibilities. They could have great answers, some of which you might even be able to verify. But you can also directly measure that aptitude. Pick something of the role that the candidate hasn't yet done. Ask them to do some research on their own and return with the results of how they applied that new knowledge to a specific problem or task you gave them.

Curiosity is a primary requisite for the ability to solve problems. I've often simply asked candidates, "What are you curious about? Are there events or things that make you wonder?" If someone doesn't have anything they wonder about, that's not a good sign for being able to resourcefully apply logic to novel challenges and invent new solutions.

Hopefully they are curious about matters related to their career.

The candidate might say "I'm curious about renewable energy technologies." Great. Then you ask, "What about renewable energy technologies make you curious?" They respond, "You know, it's kind of cool, how, y'know, we can create energy from wind and, like, solar." You reply, "Yes, it is cool. But what about those cool technologies raises your curiosity?" If that stumps them, you've just done a depth sounding of their ability to investigate possible actions to take to solve a challenge.

Live demonstration of their abilities is a great way to get an accurate assessment quickly. It also gives the candidate an example of the kind of work they would be doing if they are offered the role. It can test someone's ability to succeed in a task they've never done before. You may have candidates who have never constructed an Enterprise Risk Management program, for example, but that is one of the accountabilities you have established for a specific role. You could ask candidates to do their own research and respond within a time frame they determine (they set the date, not you) with a recommendation about the contents, approach, and method of completing the objective. You wouldn't expect a perfect response, but you can find out how adept the candidates are in educating themselves on new areas of responsibility, and in what time frame, to produce a quality result. You also find out if they can accurately forecast the time required, i.e., whether they can hit the deadline they imposed on themselves.

Motivation is another key area of course. The first question is how motivated are they to pursue the opportunity? Secondly, how motivated are they to perform the role over a years-long period of time? If a candidate balks at the behavioral demonstrations or assignments, it's a clue that they may not be capable of the role. They may not really want the job enough. Or their ego won't permit them to stoop to demonstrating their abilities. In any case, it's not a good indicator of future success.

When we were recruiting for HR leaders on behalf of clients at HRG, for example, we used a 60-question knowledge test with open-ended essay questions for some of the responses, as part of our candidate evaluation queries. Many candidates declined to complete the assignment, some even after they agreed to it. The best candidates loved it. They couldn't wait to show what they could do. Even if they weren't hired, they stayed active in our candidate pool for future opportunities.

Many times, you will hear a hiring manager say, "I can't afford to waste time training someone. I need a person who can hit the ground running." This is something spoken by leaders who don't want to work that hard at helping others succeed, and who don't recognize that no matter what someone's capabilities are, everyone needs support, guidance and training as they enter a role in a new organization. Even "seasoned" professionals.

Such a response from the hiring manager also reveals that they don't understand motivation. How motivated do you think someone will be to enter a role that they can do in their sleep, that offers no challenges or new experiences? They might accept the job out of practical necessity, but that's not an enduringly positive motivation.

What I have found in my own entrepreneurial path, and I would say was true at WD-40 Company as well, is that people who have high aptitude for professional growth and a strong desire to achieve mastery in a role they haven't yet done are far more motivated to increase their contributions and abilities, and they are satisfied in the role for far longer, than someone who has been there and done that for years. If such an adept novice is also working for a true servant leader who invests in their growth alongside them, incredible things are accomplished. Engagement goes through the roof and stays there for a long time.

You can test motivation early, during the application process. At WD-40 Company, when we were recruiting for General Counsel externally because we had not succeeded in developing an internal candidate, the first step for applicants along with the submission of their resume and completion of an application was to respond to specific questions about how their abilities and experiences both fit the role and did *not* fit the role. No candidate was expected to match all aspects of the position. It wasn't possible. Those who failed to self-identify the areas that were not directly matched between their abilities and the role demonstrated that they were not willing to be objective, honest and transparent in pursuing whether there was a match. The general counsel role had to be performed by a person with those characteristics, to be aligned with the company's values and the expectations of the function. In truth, objectivity, honesty, and transparency are character traits that are required of *every* role at WD-40 Company. Being willing to be honest about one's abilities and viewpoints is an indicator of both motivations and character.

Applicants who responded well to the first step were then given a set of seven follow up queries, to learn how they think about problems and business challenges in a legal context, what their philosophy was about the role of a general counsel in a public company, how well they could communicate in written form, how they viewed the preferable structure of legal services in a global, decentralized organization, and other topics. While these questions revealed more about the candidate's competencies, as well as their views of how to perform the role best, the process also measured how motivated they were to earn an interview. Ego-driven candidates, or those who were just casually fishing for opportunities, fell out at that stage.

Based on either non-responsiveness or quality of responses, the fallout rate between these two pre-interview steps and the first interview was 96%. There were 345 applicants, of which 241 completed the first set of questions. Out of that group, 48 were invited to complete the second set of queries. Out of that group 16 were invited to the first interview. Content-valid queries and behavioral demonstrations of "fit" continued through to the finalist interviews.

This process reduced the amount of wasted time in evaluating a huge number of initial candidates to almost nothing. This simple approach measured competencies, values alignment, and motivation simultaneously. The interview process continued with the core query methodology. We had three finalists and the successful candidate who was offered the role has turned out to be a great new tribe mate.

In summary:

- Define the role carefully and fully: purpose, functions, competencies, and accountabilities.
- Identify the behavioral attributes of character that correlate to success on the job and "fit" to organizational values.
- Compose queries that provide behavioral evidence of competencies, motivation, fit to the culture and the specific role; apply those queries across all candidates without fail. If you don't use the same yardstick, you can't compare candidates accurately.
- "When in doubt, don't". This means if you have reservations or concerns about a candidate deeper in the evaluation process, don't decide until you get behavioral evidence to either support or resolve your concern. Without obtaining confirming evidence validating your concern, you might miss a great candidate simply because of a misunderstanding or a false conclusion on your part.
- Take your time; don't take short-cuts along the way. Don't make a hiring decision on a few hours of interactions with people. How much analysis do you do to decide whether to make an offer on a house? Why would you do less in making hiring decisions when the impact is similarly years long?

The last point deserves illumination. One of the most important aspects of successful recruiting is to be doing it continually, whether you have an existing opening for the role or not. You've heard the axiom, "Don't shop when you're hungry". This applies to recruiting. If you wait until you have an opening to begin sourcing candidates, you are likely intent upon filling the role as quickly as possible because there will be a financial loss for as long as the position remains vacant, or others will be over-burdened. This condition increases the chances that you'll make allowances for candidates who may not fit, or you won't see the negative evidence in front of you because you want to hire someone badly. The more interactions you have with someone, over time, the more behavioral evidence you will have as to whether the person is a good fit.

For every business I created, I interviewed people every month, irrespective of a current need. I called it the "If-When" interview. The purpose was to determine "if" there was a match between the candidate and my company. Should the answer be mutually "yes", then the remaining question was "when" we could join together. At HRG, I hired a Director of Organization Development Services ten years after our first "If-When" discussion. He was phenomenal. And I always had at least a few candidates I could offer a role to when business grew to the point that I needed to expand. That accelerated our growth much faster than if I didn't start recruiting until the need arrived. Getting to know someone over a longer period resulted in a much higher chance of making the right decision as to who should be invited to join us. Having candidates at the ready also prevented me from avoiding difficult but critical discussions with people who were not contributing as needed; I never felt I was held hostage because I couldn't afford a vacancy.

You might think that people wouldn't be interested in the "If-When" interview. I never had someone decline. They often felt flattered that they were being asked to explore the possibilities. They entered the discussion without the goal-orientation of a candidate for a known opening; it was much more relaxed and exploratory. We each were kicking each other's tires and enjoying the process along the way.

After you've invited someone to join you, with the best possible evidence of likely success and longevity, now you have the possibility of this new person feeling engaged over time, and therefore becoming a strong, long-term contributor to the organization, someone you will enjoy working with. What you do after they are inside the door will help or hurt that possibility. This is now the responsibility of leadership, starting with the person who did the hiring, following your leadership philosophy and methods.

At WD-40 Company we would have new tribe member orientation that included everyone hired in the last few months. It was a great time to reconnect with people who we met during the interviewing process, see how they were doing, answer questions, etc. Senior leaders from every major functional area would participate. Garry would join as many of those orientation meetings as his travel schedule allowed. He would always ask this question: "So, did we lie to you?"

He wanted to know if what they experienced about our company, our values, our culture, our purpose, the role they were offered, etc., was as advertised during their candidacy. What a great question to ask, and ask early, in a new person's life with your organization. You can't correct a misconception, or fix a previously unknown flaw in the culture, if you don't ask this question.

If all this seems to you like a lot of thought and care, a lot of work, you are correct. Hiring well is the same challenge as building a house. Hiring is the foundation for everything else. How much care do you put into a building's foundation, so that the walls are supported, straight and true? If the walls aren't constructed properly, how well will the doors and windows fit? How strong will the roof be?

When I arrived as a tribe member at WD-40 Company, I knew that we should create a strong candidate sourcing capability. By establishing the internal ability to source and evaluate candidates, we dramatically reduced the need to use fee-based external recruiters around the world. At the same time, the quality of our hiring decisions improved a lot. We would employ contract sourcing professionals to augment our internal team during high-demand periods, but we did not out-source candidate evaluation methodology. The contract recruiters were expected to apply the same content-valid tools and methods we used internally.

There is a lot more that can be said about building your reputation as a preferred employer through these and other actions, which will make your company a known, positive attraction for candidates. Most important, however, is the truth of your culture, its authenticity. Focus on that. Word will get out.

Just as important as who you hire is the question of who you promote, especially into leadership roles. You may have hired a great person who thrived as an individual contributor but may not be capable of leading in the way that creates both engagement and results. The same principles of candidate evaluation that apply to your hiring process are applicable to the question of who to invite to be a leader. It's a mistake to assume that a current employee who demonstrates competency, character, values alignment, motivation, and team-orientation in their work history with your company will also be the same in a leadership role. The odds might be good, but there's a certain chance that the new role and dynamics of leadership will bring out dysfunctional behaviors in a person, particularly if it is the first time they have been accountable for others as a leader.

Often, a new leader will revert to parental behavior that they learned by observing their mother and father. Or they will emulate strong characters they encountered over their career, even if they wouldn't say they admired those leaders. Or they will shy away from conflict, being uncertain about their own capabilities. Or they will want to be liked, as a primary motivation.

And sometimes, leadership can go to someone's head. Depending upon their motivation to lead, as discussed earlier, they could be thinking, "Finally! Now I can get things done *my* way!" They suddenly feel powerful and unconcerned about others' opinions.

Developing leaders includes giving them opportunities to lead without the accountability for making decisions about people, such as project leadership, coordinating a multi-functional team or leading a meeting. If they can demonstrate the ability to lead others through influence rather than authority, guiding groups to achieve without issuing commands, they are more likely able to lead similarly when formal authority is assigned.

The absolute killer of a culture is promoting someone into leadership or advancing them to higher levels of accountability within leadership, who does not live your values, and does not demonstrate the type of leadership that increases engagement of others. Take the time you need to be as sure as you can before you offer leadership to anyone, whether they are an external candidate or a current member of your organization.

BEING A COACH

Assuming you have done well in deciding who to invite to join you, the next most important factor is how you interact with them after they start work. If you are a servant leader, someone who believes their primary objective in leading others is to catalyze their success and growth, you will be adopting the role of a coach and mentor.

A successful coach's mindset is focused on the person being coached. I won't repeat the previous sections on the role of a leader, so just know that those concepts are embedded in the principles I'll offer here. Remember that the single most common reason people resign from their job is due to a poor relationship they have with their immediate leader. Intentionally making that relationship productive, positive, and mutually satisfying is another critical element in creating high engagement. "Positive lasting memories."

I'll assume that you haven't felt significant disagreement with the ideas presented so far in this book. You're still reading, presumably, right?

Therefore, the next question to ask yourself is, "How do I behave as a coach?"

I could be flippant and just say, "Read Garry's and Ken Blanchard's book." And you should, of course. But I'll offer some ideas that are complementary to the great ideas you'll find in "Helping People Win at Work".

Assuming you have hired well, the next most common reason why people don't succeed in a role is that expectations are not clear. If you've carefully and accurately done the work to define the role—the purpose, functions, competencies, and characteristics required—then you will have already solved for most of this challenge. But even if you have done that, there is still an opportunity to send someone off in the wrong direction, or no direction.

With any new person, the first goal is to quickly tool them up to start making contributions. Literally. They need the tools required for their role. They need access to systems and applications. They need to know who does what and who to go to for specific functional aspects of their job. They need to understand the history related to their accountabilities, what has gone right and what has gone wrong. They need to know immediate priorities. They need organizational knowledge about strategies, objectives, challenges, and timelines. They need to be introduced personally to people with whom they will work if they didn't meet them during the interview process. They need time to build trust and the foundations of an enduring relationship with their teammates.

A new person also needs frequent access to you, their coach. Much more frequently in the early days, of course, than after they have settled into their position, capable of more autonomous action. As coach, you can help them course-correct before they get moving too fast in the wrong direction.

If you're sailing from San Francisco to Hawaii, and your compass point is off by three minutes, you'll miss the islands by many miles. Better to make small adjustments sooner than later.

Assuming you have launched your new person's boat well, time will pass, and you will begin to see where they need development. You may have identified some areas during the interview and evaluation process already.

Since a leader is a teacher, the approach is to identify what a person must be trained on, and what they need coaching on. Training is the approach to apply when a person has not yet mastered the basics of any given responsibility or functional task. They need the facts, the methods, the processes, the information, the history, etc. They need practice building skills through repetitive application of the basics.

Once a person has mastered the basics, now it's time to allow them more freedom to apply their knowledge and skills to accomplishing objectives, while the coach stays on the sidelines to guide them when they encounter a hurdle or challenge that they are unsure of. The coach's job is to help them solve their own problems with guidance, not do it for them. They will make mistakes. And they will learn more from their mistakes than from their successes.

This approach is taught in the Situational Leadership courses from Blanchard, a great way to think about what kind of leadership is required. It also provides the coach and their team member with a common language of how to talk about the very personal matters of capabilities, competencies, and ability to contribute.

Every person needs both training and coaching, including tenured professionals and experienced leaders. And as I like to say, "We're all white belts at something".

When I joined WD-40 Company, I and my colleagues at HRG had already worked with the organization as a client for eleven years. I soon found out how much I didn't know. Even with decades of work experience in directly related topics, I was not fully competent in my role, in my opinion, until three years after I started. I had so much to learn about the business, how it differed in various geographies, the people with whom I needed to partner, the functional accountabilities that you don't get exposed to as an external advisor. Some learning was episodic, such as preparing for and conducting meetings with the compensation committee. Those meetings occurred three or four times a year, with one being the most important, after the close of the fiscal year. I needed multiple times at bat to get better at my swing. That took a few years.

Every person is developing in some way. So, their coach needs to understand where training is required, and where coaching is needed after training is complete. Often, mistakes made by coaches relate to thinking one is needed when it's really the other. If you keep training someone who already has the basics down pat, they will be bored, frustrated, and irritated. If you move to coaching before they have the basics wired, they will be confused, nervous and unsure of themselves.

A common mistake coaches make is to assume a "senior" person only needs coaching. That is often wishful thinking. It would be so nice not to have to train someone, saving much time and effort, right? Even now, working as an external advisor to several CEOs, they relate experiences that are similar; hiring a seemingly capable leader, letting them loose to accomplish great things, only to find that they had holes in their competencies that needed filling.

Teaching is a continual requirement, for both training basics and for coaching. Done well, with "students" who have the requisite aptitude, character, and motivation, much can be accomplished while providing positive experiences for everyone. But sometimes, people either can't or won't develop.

A person might start out as a good match to the organization and their role, but life changes for them and their desire to continue to grow wanes. Or they might reach their personal limit of growth, even as the organization's needs continue to advance. Or you might discover that under stress or temptation, a person's character is pliable.

Again, to quote Garry, "Coaching is about being tough-minded and tender-hearted. The genius is in the 'and'".

First, the tender-hearted part. The best coaches I've had or observed simply care about the people they are coaching. What happens to them matters to the coach. Their successes are celebrated by the coach, who feels pride in their accomplishments. When they stumble, the coach feels personal accountability and a strong desire to redouble coaching efforts to help them recover. A good coach doesn't act like a parent, however. The relationship is truly one of equal and accountable adults, with different roles. A coach is a person who offers their knowledge, advice, and guidance so that someone else can advance along their chosen life path, to accomplish what they have decided to pursue. A coach doesn't "want it" more than the person they are coaching. A coach is a catalyst for someone else to achieve what they are committed to achieving.

With that type of relationship, a coach is also a source of truth. Coaches cannot ignore the behavioral facts and still fulfill the responsibility of being a catalyst for growth. It takes courage, i.e., a "tough mind" to be able to put aside the discomfort of engaging in possibly difficult or contentious truth-telling, for the benefit of a person's development and success.

One of my early mentors was my boss at Martin Marietta Aluminum, a huge factory in Torrance, California. It was 1979. Louis Paglialonga was head of industrial relations at the 2,000 employee, unionized aluminum fabrication facility which held gargantuan machines under 40 acres of roof. When you walked through the factory, it was like Dante's inferno, black and sooty with molten metal everywhere.

One day at lunch with Lou and others, I was complaining that my workload was ten times more than a colleague's. I had an average of 200 open requisitions at any given time for planning, production, maintenance, and tooling, while Dominic only had 10 professional and managerial roles open. And Dominic was using external headhunters. I was whining. Lou, who was caring and kind to me as a rule, looked straight at me and said, "You're not doing half of what you should be. Why don't you focus on your own work and quit worrying about everybody else?"

That was my first experience of what I've come to call the Velvet Two-by-Four. It's a loving whack upside the head, to knock away the self-centered filter that prevented seeing the truth. I didn't know how hard it was to find engineers, production managers and senior executives. I just looked at the numbers, making the dumb assumption that all positions were equal tasks for recruiting. Humbled and now awake, I redoubled my efforts. I figured out a way to increase candidate volume and reduce the evaluation time required, a method that I still apply today. I hired 200 people in half the previous time frame required, increased the quality of people we brought on, which resulted in reduction of turnover by 50%, dropping our average shop openings to 100 at any given time.

Lou was the embodiment of Garry's "tough-minded and tender-hearted" coach. Lou really cared about me, and everyone else as well, including Dominic. Lou told me the truth. I then had to decide whether to respond to the challenge or continue to wallow in my self-righteous indignation. I took what Lou said to heart because I *knew* he cared about me.

It's not easy to tell people the truth. They might resist it, deny it, even accuse you of being a poor coach. It's not fun to learn that your coach thinks you are not as capable as you need to be, or as capable as you think you are. But a good coach knows that it does no one a favor to ignore such truth, especially the person who needs to hear it.

Coaches who truly care about people understand this. They accept the responsibility to be factual and honest with those whom they coach. Their character, their mind is "tough" in that they don't fear the negative reaction from someone who needs to hear the truth. They care more about helping someone succeed than they fear a difficult, emotional conversation with someone. Such a leader sacrifices their own comfort so that someone else has a chance to face reality and decide what course they will commit to. Facing reality can be scary. But it doesn't have to be.

At WD-40 Company, Garry introduced the idea of "learning moments". A learning moment is a positive or negative outcome of some action or decision that is openly and freely shared to benefit all people. Intelligent mistakes, based on hard work and failed outcomes, are to be celebrated. Everybody has learning moments.

A couple of years after I joined WD-40 Company, I made the decision to purchase an HR information system that would allow us to globally understand our population, labor costs, demographics, and other important elements of our workforce. It would provide the capability to plan various scenarios related to growth. It would create an efficient, visible, and auditable method for making compensation changes. It would dramatically reduce the hours required to produce required reporting. We had gotten outside guidance on which systems to consider. I had involved my team in the exploration. I took all input under consideration, but the decision was mine to make.

Based on the recommendations of our systems consultant and our collective analysis, I chose a platform and we proceeded to begin implementation. One year into the project, we had encountered many issues with the system. It was not operating as advertised. We had dedicated significant time and money to the project. My brave leader of compensation and HR systems, Kimberly, came to me one day and said, "If we continue to try to implement this system, we will have a disaster when we start the migration to other countries." She was right.

Kimberly and I first tried to work with the publisher of the HR information system. We flew to the east coast and met with their CEO and senior leaders. At WD-40 Company, you don't begin a vendor relationship lightly, and you don't leave it without being honest about the issues and trying to resolve them. That meeting proved to us that there was zero chance of making the system work for us.

I went to Garry and our CFO, Jay Rembolt, and explained the problem. I said we needed to change to a different system that we had found and more thoroughly vetted, which would extend our implementation time and triple the cost, both on installation and as an ongoing subscription. They listened carefully, and said, "Ok. Will you share your learning moment at our next senior leadership meeting?"

I did just that, explaining the situation to all 30 leaders who gathered two or three times a year from around the world, at our meeting in San Diego. After my presentation, one leader asked, "What did you learn?" I replied, "I was penny wise and pound foolish." That was the last anyone ever said about it. Kimberly and I went on to map out the implementation plan with a system which is working great, at every office of the company from Shanghai to London, from Australia to Toronto.

That was my first direct experience with the philosophy of "learning moments", as a tribe member of the company. The power of this philosophy is hard to over-state.

When people are not afraid to either make well-meaning mistakes nor to reveal them publicly, learning is dramatically accelerated. If people are not afraid, they are not risk averse.

People will volunteer, take on assignments they may have never done before and immediately disclose issues without trying to cover them up. Engagement is dramatically amplified.

Being accountable for someone else's life and livelihood, being a coach, is a sober and serious responsibility. People who do it well should be recognized. At WD-40 Company my colleagues and I created the Golden Flask Award. The vessel referred to is an Erlenmeyer flask common to scientists. We chose that image as the emblem of our Leadership Laboratory. We made up gold-plated pins in the shape of that flask. When a leader applied the principles of leadership taught in the Lab in a difficult challenge of courageous leadership, we would first gain approval from that leader's coach and then call the leader to meet.

The leader, their coach, and members of the faculty of Leadership Lab would convene. We didn't tell the recipient why we were meeting in advance. We would then describe the courageous actions the leader had taken, how they applied the principles from the Lab and the positive outcome they achieved on behalf of the entire organization with the best interests of all involved front of mind for them. We highlighted why they deserved recognition for being "tough-minded and tender-hearted". We gave them a commemorative description of the award, and the gold-plated Erlenmeyer flask pin. At company events you would see people wearing their golden flask pin proudly. It was a small but important way to show appreciation and recognition for coaches being truly the kind of leaders who could put aside their own sense of safety to do what was right for their tribe member and for the company.

It's possible that a coach is not the right person to be coaching someone for whom they are responsible. That doesn't relieve them of the responsibility. The coach might need to call in a specialist or ask another leader for assistance in providing the training or coaching needed. Recognizing that need takes self-awareness and humility. When others see such humility, they will also feel safer to reveal where they are not completely competent themselves.

A key to getting better at being a coach (or being a capable person in general) is healthy self-skepticism. As my Grandpa used to say, "I don't believe half the things I think." He was decades ahead of the neuroscience that has proven none of us completely know our own mind.

Our brains are composed of three levels of activity, only one of which is accessible consciously. The most straightforward way to describe the conscious mind state is the part of our mind that we can talk about. It incorporates our present sensory awareness and the thoughts and feelings we are having in the moment which we can describe in language. Right now, I'm aware of the light in this office, the sound of a jet high above, the sound of the keys clicking as I type, the sense of cold on my bare feet in my slippers, the tinnitus in my ears, the dove's low cooing in the tree outside and my choice of words as I type. I can feel the keyboard under the tips of my fingers. I sense the air temperature on my bare arms and face. I am thinking of the words that will immediately appear on the screen in front of me.

My unconscious mind is comprised of thoughts, actions and biases that used to be conscious, but are now so habitual I'm not aware of them. In ninth grade I learned how to type. Now as I write these words, I no longer need to consciously choose which finger goes to which button. I just think of the word and my fingers fly accurately. Well, most of the time.

Unconscious mind activities are going on all the time. They are the repository of our habitual behavior, the assimilated "rules" of society that we have chosen to follow, our biases and preferences, our values, physical skills, and our habits.

A third level of mind is our sub-conscious, the part of our mind's activities that are not conscious and may never have been. This is the realm of emotions, survival systems and behaviors that developed before we acquired the ability of language.

If we accept that we have mind activities which affect our behaviors, and which are not immediately accessible to our awareness, then we must continually acknowledge that we should question our own beliefs, opinions, and behaviors. This is another reason why self-report personality inventory results should be viewed skeptically.

Far from being a detriment, this self-skepticism opens whole new ways of exploring the world, and of accomplishing what we want to accomplish. As a coach, when you demonstrate such openness to explore your own thoughts, you provide a powerful example for others who you may be encouraging to dig deeper into their motivations, their ability to perform and their beliefs about what they can or cannot do.

Garry was the first CEO I encountered who demonstrated self-skepticism openly, publicly, in the moment. We would be discussing some topic, wrestling with the issue, sharing our thoughts. Garry would say something firmly and confidently, as a conclusion to the open question, as if he had arrived at the end of his deliberations and strongly declared the answer.

Then he would look out the window and say, "Now, why do I think that...?" He was examining why and how he had come to that opinion or conclusion, questioning the validity of the definitive statement he had made just seconds prior. That demonstration of being skeptical of one's own powerful views gave everyone around him the permission to firmly state a position in one moment, and then change it in another, if there was reason to question one's own thoughts, if the assumptions were no longer valid, if the facts changed.

Can you see how powerful that example was? It made it easy for people to change their minds when new information was discovered, or when someone realized their deeply held opinion was based on flawed logic or experiences that weren't relevant. People would less likely get stuck defending their position when it was wrong, for fear of appearing wishy washy or weak. It was a demonstration of the learning mentality in real time.

Coaches are accountable for ensuring others learn and grow, succeeding in their chosen field and role. To do so, coaches must exhibit continual learning themselves. Yet another quote from Garry: "The three most powerful words I have learned are 'I don't know'". Garry modeled the leader who is continually learning, who is not afraid to say they didn't know. I have participated in a lot of board meetings and earnings calls at WD-40 Company. I'll never forget one such earnings call when a significant investor's representative asked Garry what the company was going to do to react to the onset of the

Great Recession and how the company would fare in 2009. Most CEOs would have pulled together some bland assurances and false confidence to respond. Garry said, "I don't know what specific actions we will need to take at the moment. We are gathering the facts and evaluating possible courses of action. All I can tell you at this time is that we're not going to panic. Stay tuned. We'll keep you informed."

By his example, Garry was teaching us all to be open to changing our minds, with humility and constant learning, especially about ourselves. He taught us that saying "I don't know" was a valid answer to a question. That's what a coach does to help others evolve.

We all have examples of the kind of leaders who inspired us, who believed in us more than we believed in ourselves, who invested time and energy on our behalf. Be that leader. As CEO, you have the primary impact on every other leader in your organization. As you behave, so will others. If you want leaders who can teach, who can tell people the truth with care and candor, who can inspire, you must model that behavior yourself. You won't be perfect at it, but again, perfection is not the standard. Just keep getting better at it. Remember that *your organization cannot evolve any faster than you do.*

ACCOUNTABLE ADULTS

Wouldn't you love it if your company's people behaved this way? No victim's mindset. No blaming others. No hiding from responsibility for mistakes. No whining. Focused attention on finding solutions, applying objectivity and facts, rather than speculation and anger.

Achieving such a cultural norm doesn't happen without intention.

As always, it starts with you, the business leader, and then extends to all your other leaders. You must ask yourself if you personally are behaving as an accountable adult. But what exactly is the behavior needed, and how do you demonstrate it?

As introduced in the last chapter, there are three mind states in all of us. Sigmund Freud, a physician who established the psychoanalytic approach to clinical therapy, called these mind states the *id*, the *ego* and the *superego*. In Freud's theory of psychoanalysis, the *id* was the primitive, early part of the mind, dominant from the prenatal stage up until about age seven. This mind state set up the internal conditions for later development, and was focused on physiological safety, security. It was primarily influenced by one's parents and early experiences between the womb and early childhood.

The *ego* was the self-conscious part of the mind, focused on creating a self-image that was preferred, gaining rewards, and avoiding negative consequences. The *ego* is the organized, realistic agent that mediates between *id* and *superego*.

The *superego* was the part of the mind that attempted to control the id and the ego, comprised of societal rules and morals learned from one's parents and other authority figures.

Some of Freud's theories have not stood the test of time and have been replaced by more enduring principles supported by neuroscience, biology, and experimental evidence. But it is interesting that the more we learn about the functioning of the human brain, we find psychophysiological correlates to Freud's three mind states.

The *id* maps well in concept to two sub-systems in our brains. One is the "hind brain" or "reptilian brain" structure in humans, so called because the physical structure and operation of this part of the human brain is very similar to the entire brain found in reptiles. This area of the brain is focused on survival and is the triggering source for "fight-flight-freeze" responses to threats. The other structure is the "mid-brain", comprised primarily of the limbic system, which is where emotions, appetites for rewards and memory formation are regulated.

The hind brain and the limbic system are the dominant forms of thought for all of us, from the time our brains are largely formed in the womb to the point of our ability to develop the capacity for language.

The *ego* and *superego* are developed as the brain continues to grow after birth, when the cortex is formed more fully and the connectivity of neurons with glial networks proliferates. The cortex isn't complete, physiologically, until about age 22-25. The part of the cortex that finishes construction last is the pre-frontal cortex, the section of our brain just behind our forehead. This segment of the brain is where "executive" functions of impulse control, rationality and logic are derived.

As we have impactful life experiences that connect to our emotions and our needs for safety and security, and as we absorb the rules of life while we are moving through childhood into adulthood, much of our behavior moves from the aware, conscious mind state to the unconscious. The unconscious mind also includes skills and habits of behavior that used to be conscious but have now become automatic in how they are called upon in daily life. This is how the *superego* is created, as an unconscious set of behavioral habits and biases, that used to be conscious, moving from the *ego* to the *superego*.

In 1957, a psychiatrist named Dr. Eric Berne introduced a transactional model of the mind, modernizing Freud's terminology, which allowed a more practical and behaviorally based structure of the theory. Below, Dr. Berne's mind states are compared to Freud's terms, the relevant neurophysiological anatomy and the operational level of thought associated with each state.

Freud	**Physical Brain Structures***	**Operational State**	**Dr. Berne**
Superego	Cortex and Cerebellum	Unconscious	Parent

| *Ego* | Pre-frontal Cortex & Temporal Lobe | Conscious | Adult |
| *Id* | Hindbrain & Limbic System | Sub-conscious | Child |

[* These categorizations are simplifications; the brain is an integrated system that is still being discovered, with anatomical and functional dependencies of a complex nature.]

Dr. Berne chose his terminology because the terms best described the human experience of being in such mind states and how behavior was exhibited. The Leadership Laboratory at WD-40 Company teaches these concepts because they are extremely useful in navigating leadership challenges and resolving interpersonal conflicts.

All three mind states are operating simultaneously, and are critical to a healthy, happy human experience of life. The child mind state is the source of creativity, joy, playfulness, and wonder. The parent mind state is protective and prepares for calamities. The adult mind state is efficient and effective in objectively solving problems, examining the facts, and choosing directions. The adult mind state can inhibit "child" impulses and desires.

Each can be more dominant in some people than in others; we are all unique. And mind states may be differently active depending on the experiential context. The most important mind state to develop, to be a self-accountable person, is the adult mind state, the one that is the most objective, rational, logical, and capable of regulating emotional reactions, such as anger or fear. It must be remembered, however, that all three mind states are essential in both fulfilling chosen responsibilities but also in being a whole, integrated human being.

The first step in improving your culture of accountability as a leader is to understand these mind states and to cultivate your ability to *choose to operate* from each when it is necessary and constructive.

If you lead only from the parent mind state, you could either be too accommodative (the nurturing, protective and enabling parent) or too critical (the judgmental, punishing parent). And if you act as a parent, treating people like children, Dr. Berne showed that people will likely respond as expected. They will react from their child mind state, being rebellious and resistive, or contrite and self-loathing, when judged. They might learn helplessness if you parentally protect them from consequences, which is the road to a victim's mindset.

If you lead primarily from your child mind state, the reaction you get in response will either be from their child mind state (they want to play with you or fight with you) or from their parent (they want to change *your* behavior).

If you lead from your objective, non-judgmental adult mind state, addressing their adult, it is more likely that they will respond in kind, applying reason, logic and openness to the challenge or task at hand.

There is so much more to be said about this model of understanding the psychology of leadership and how you can apply it to great effect. In fact, every leader eventually must become a bit of a psychologist, whether they get a formal education in it or not. Many great leaders know this dynamic intuitively, built from their own keen eye, life experiences and a strong desire to create a cohesive, successful organization.

Let's assume you adopt this construct and begin to apply it. You lead, especially in challenging times or when someone needs corrective guidance, from the adult mind state. How then do you engage others to emulate the accountable, adult state of mind?

It has been said that leadership is more about the questions you ask, than the statements you make. In fact, Socrates established an entire school of thought about proper education methods, in the fourth century BCE. The "Socratic method" was based on inquiry, not lecture. That method elicits responses from the rational, "adult" mind state.

Here is a tool we taught at WD-40 Company in the Leadership Laboratory, to be applied when someone required coaching and guidance to improve their performance. It is a sequence of questions that may be used serially as shown, or partially, depending upon the needs of the moment. The questions are posed from the leader's "adult" mind state and are addressed to the "adult" mind state of the other person, requiring the respondent to make a conscious choice in how to reply. If delivered without the non-verbal and tonal elements found in either the "parent" or "child" mind states, they are likely to elicit the accountable responses of the "adult":

1. <u>What</u> do you believe you are accountable for?
2. <u>Why</u> are you (or are you not) committed to achieving those accountabilities?

3. <u>Can</u> you accomplish the (goal, task, objective, etc.) that you are accountable for?

4. If not, <u>what do you need</u>, to be able to accomplish it?

5. <u>Will</u> you achieve the (goal, task, objective, etc.)?

6. What is your <u>plan</u> for achieving the (goal, task, objective, etc.)?

7. <u>What do you expect</u> of me and or others as part of that plan?

8. <u>How will you know</u> if your plan is, or is not working?

9. <u>What is your backup plan</u> for accomplishing the (goal, task, objective) should your original plan not work?

10. (If the person did not achieve the results they committed to) <u>What did you learn</u> and <u>how will you approach this same type of challenge differently</u> next time?

By asking such questions, the likely result is that of an accountable adult choosing how to respond, rather than submitting to threats or rewards. You may find that there is a disconnect between what you believe the person is accountable for and what they understand expectations to be. You may find that they don't have the motivation to attempt to achieve the objectives. You may find they just don't have a plan and are stumped as to how to proceed. If the leader asking these questions has truly demonstrated that they care about the person, the odds are even higher that the result of this inquiry will be honest and accountable in response. What you find out by asking such questions will inform your decisions about what to do next as their leader. You might simply have to clarify the goals. Or you might need to go back to training basics, a step you could have missed. Or you may find that the person just doesn't want to do the role anymore, so you can work with them to find a path of heart for their future, in or out of the organization.

This approach of communicating with people increases the odds of building an accountable culture where people do not behave as victims. Coupled with this idea is the ultimate view that most business owners come to adopt for themselves: "There are lots of reasons. There are no excuses." A business owner knows that the only place to look when things go wrong is the mirror. An excuse relieves someone from accountability. The adult in us knows that when we accept a responsibility, there is no escape clause. So, we had better be certain we want to accept the responsibility in the first place.

Therefore, accountable people don't say "yes" to everything. They are conservative when deadlines or metrics are established. They analyze the path to success and their own capabilities carefully before they agree or commit to achieving a goal. Most accountable people try to under-promise and over-deliver. They don't send a text message 20 minutes before a meeting that they agreed to, asking where the meeting is, hoping not to hear something back, so they have an excuse for not showing up. Yes, I've known people who have done exactly that. And worse. So have you.

Asking questions as a means of leading applies to strong performers as well. There is nothing more motivating than to be talking with your leader about a big company challenge, and they lean in to ask, "What do *you* think?" with deep interest. To be asked one's advice by one's coach is a sign of respect and trust. People feel truly valued when this happens. It must be authentic; people smell phony-ness a long way off.

You, the CEO, must really want to know what they think, for your own benefit.

Adult behavior in leaders will elicit adult responses and engagement with others. Your own approach to interactive inquiry will determine the odds of others adopting the same mindset. Here's an example of an exchange, in two forms:

Frank is meeting with his leader, his coach, and says, "I know you spend regular time with Linda, but you don't have one-on-one meetings with me. Why does Linda get more of your time for development than I do?"

The leader, Andre, replies, "Well, I've been really busy. I have a hard time keeping up with emails, as I'm sure you do as well, and all these meetings. Linda and I have been working on a specific objective that is a priority for our department. I'm sorry you feel that I haven't devoted enough time to you. I'll try my best to rectify that."

This exchange is a child-parent interaction: whining child, apologetic and guilty parent. Let's try it again.

Frank says, "I know you spend regular time with Linda, but you don't have one-on-one meetings with me. Why does Linda get more of your time for development than I do?"

Andre replies, "Would you like to spend more time with me? What would you like to be the reason we meet?"

Frank replies, "Well, I just want to learn from you and share what I've been accomplishing. I'd like to learn about opportunities that might be coming up."

Andre says, "So you're interested in growing and exploring ways to advance in your career?"

Frank says, "Yes."

Andre says, "That's great. You have access to my calendar. Feel free to schedule a day and time we can spend an hour or two to begin this discussion. Please come prepared to describe your career objectives, what areas of competency you want to grow in and how you'd like to invest in your own development. I'm looking forward to it."

See the difference? It takes practice and self-awareness for a leader to not fall into the unconscious parent or child mind states when such interactions occur. Habits are hard to break, as we all know, because they have been reinforced over periods of years.

I was on the phone yesterday with the CEO of an e-commerce retail and distribution platform. He was describing a meeting he had with his senior leadership team. The dynamics were that of a group of children complaining to their Dad, who felt guilty for not being a better parent, and resentful that they didn't recognize all his hard work trying to provide for them. His leadership team has an average of 30 years of experience each; the child mind state lives in us all, no matter how many years we have on the planet.

I worked with the CEO to script alternatives to the replies he provided at the meeting, so that he stayed out of the nurturing, remorseful parent mind state and remained in the adult state, addressing their adult mind state. When you interact with others respectfully, directly, factually and with a willingness to take accountability yourself, they will more likely respond in kind.

At WD-40 Company we had the Maniac Pledge, to remind us of the need to be self-accountable, to act like adults:

The Maniac Pledge

"I am responsible for taking action, asking questions, getting answers and making decisions. I won't wait for someone to tell me. If I need to know, I am responsible for asking. I have no right to be offended that I 'didn't get this sooner'. If I am doing something others should know about, I am responsible for telling them."

Remember that everyone has a choice in how they behave. I highly recommend a book we used as reference in our Leadership Laboratory. It's called "Man's Search for Meaning" by Viktor Frankl. Frankl is the all-time heavyweight champion of accountable behavior. He was trained as a psychiatrist and neurologist. He survived three concentration camps during World War II. His book was written in his head while a prisoner. He used the time spent as a sort of sabbatical to advance his theory of meaning and its importance to human psychology, and to the ability of people to survive the death camps, starting with himself.

Frankl said that between stimulus and response, there is the human ability to pause, to think and to choose what response one wishes to make. He said that in that ability to choose is freedom, the kind that no one can take from you.

Teaching people that they can choose their actions, in any circumstance, and that it is their responsibility to do so, is key to catalyzing human capability and increasing a person's desire to engage. Your communication approach can increase the odds that people do recognize their responsibility to choose, to act, to solve their own problems, to ask for what they need, to be accountable adults. By your own example, behaving as an accountable adult, you will have a catalytic effect on everyone else around you.

"NO LYING, FAKING OR HIDING"

Garry used this phrase to bring a touchy subject into the light. Even the best people might be tempted at times to fib, withhold facts, act as if something is okay when it's not or stay out of sight during difficult interactions. Garry says that he believes most people don't consciously lie; they fake and hide out of fear. I think that's probably true in a lot of cases. Some people do choose to lie, however, and rationalize their reasons: "It's just a little lie." "I didn't lie; I only withheld the truth, to be polite." While some people choose to be deceitful, and others don't, the motivations are identical.

At the most basic level of motivation, the trunk splits into two main branches. Humans do what they do to either gain what is perceived to be a reward, or to avoid what is perceived to be a negative consequence. Or both. The evaluation of what constitutes a reward or a consequence doesn't start out as a conscious decision; it's emotional, based on our hierarchy of needs, as Maslow clearly identified. If I am underwater, running out of oxygen, my emotional drive is survival and I do whatever I can to gain the reward of air while avoiding the consequence of drowning. In that situation, another swimmer might offer me a pound of gold and it would not divert my attention in the least. If I'm instead sitting in a beach chair seaside, sipping a cool drink, thinking about how nice it would be someday to retire, I would more likely respond to the offer, to gain the more abstract reward of discretionary time and opportunity for pleasurable experiences—and avoid the consequence of possibly having to work all the way to my grave.

As we grow through childhood and into our adult life, our behaviors are shaped by our experiences. What has "worked" for us during our developmental years and beyond is reinforced and more likely to be part of our behavior patterns for the long term. A child who has been physically punished for helping themselves to a sandwich from the refrigerator will not stop being hungry. They will instead learn how to get the sandwich when no one is looking—they will hide their actions. If asked if they got into the fridge by the parent who is ready to smack them should the answer be "yes", they will convincingly say "no". If that child had been hit every time they came home with a poor grade in math, they would soon learn to cheat by taking others' work home, faking their performance.

But what about adults? Don't we grow out of our childhood fears and urges? The short answer is "no". Not without self-awareness and a deep exploration of unconscious and subconscious sources of behavior. It is said that to lie convincingly, the first person you must lie to is yourself. You must tell yourself that it's true and come to believe it. Or you must tell yourself that it's justified because you deserve the outcome you are trying to gain through lying. Or you must believe that your lie is a counter action to someone else's hurtful actions, so it's fair. To change one's pattern of applying deceit to gain rewards and avoid consequences, we must first discover our own behavior patterns, to realize that we don't know ourselves fully and to face ourselves in the mirror— without judgment.

Judging ourselves, or self-loathing, is a powerful punishment that most people will avoid at all costs. They will continue to lie to themselves and use deceit with others to preserve a self-image that they can accept. But if through introspection a person can come to understand how they developed their lying, faking, and hiding behaviors, they have a chance to accept themselves and then choose a different behavioral future. This often takes a traumatic catalyst, and it always takes courage.

When the behavior no longer provides the reward and/or avoidance of consequences previously enjoyed, perhaps even yielding the reverse, there is now emotional drive to change. When you can't lie to, fake out or hide from yourself anymore, you then must make a choice. That takes bravery, which is to act despite fear of the consequences that have been avoided for many years.

The momentum behind learned deceit is powerful. Even when self-awareness begins, a person might continue to lie, fake, and hide, out of strong habit formation. It becomes automatic. It's an unconscious habit, driven by subconscious drives for reward and avoidance of punishment. It's a survival mechanism formed over a lifetime. Very hard to stop.

An organization can create a system of behavioral norms that reduces the incidence rate of lying, faking, and hiding. The first element in that system is not hiring people who behave that way, of course. But to a certain degree, everyone is tempted at some point to get what they want, or avoid a consequence, through deceit. They say that locks keep honest people honest. Once a good person is hired, the organizational system of "locks" includes behavioral rewards for honesty in act and word. Mistakes are not punished if the person learns by the mistake, and it wasn't intentional. As mentioned before, we call them "learning moments" at WD-40 Company, and they are celebrated.

Another organizational system element is leadership's demonstration of being transparent and forthright in all communications and actions. One slippery act by a leader can be the beginning of the end of a transparent organization. Free self-disclosure of a senior leader's own errors to the organization gives others permission to own up to their own failings without punishment.

A key reason people will fib, fake or hide is if they are punished for telling the truth. If you react angrily to bad news, you will train everyone around you to hide the bad news, make up better stories or deflect accountability for results.

Finally, deceit should not be rewarded by pay raises, promotions, and opportunities. If an employee smashes through their goals and creates great profitability for the organization, but they did it by subterfuge and dishonesty, any reward that followed would tell the whole organization that lying, faking, and hiding was to be praised.

In summary, people lie, fake, and hide because:

- It's what they learned growing up; it has "worked" to get them what they wanted to gain, and avoid what they wanted to avoid, through to adulthood
- They are unaware of their own behavior patterns, motivations
- They believe their own lies and/or feel that they are justified

- It's a powerful habit that is automatic and difficult to stop, even if the person wants to
- The environment in which they live tolerates, or worse, rewards lying, faking, and hiding

Organizational leaders who understand these factors have an opportunity to systematically eliminate deceitful behavior by:

- Hiring people who have a developmental history that promoted honesty in word and action, as evidenced by demonstrated honesty in word and deed revealed during the candidate evaluation process
- Clearly demonstrating their own honesty through transparency and disclosure
- Publicly rewarding honesty, especially in admitting mistakes
- Not rewarding performance results that were based in some part on deceit
- Counseling and if necessary separating employees who exhibit the habits of lying, faking, and hiding, and don't respond to coaching

Garry openly talked about this challenge during leadership meetings, casual discussions, during Leadership Lab, wherever. Simply by bringing the topic up for open exploration, he gave us all permission to first admit that maybe we've done a little bit of fibbing, fudged a few numbers or ignored an email whose subject we hoped would die from neglect. Garry was saying, "C'mon, we know this goes on, for all of us, right? But let's be better than that. Let's help each other call it when we see it, so we can eliminate it."

TRANSPARENCY EQUALS TRUST

Let's dig a bit deeper into this subject, and why it's so crucial for creating high engagement. Transparency is the exact opposite of "lying, faking or hiding".

I'm sure you've heard someone in your work experiences say something like, "They have a hidden agenda". Or they'll speculate about why someone did or did not do something, theorizing that their motives were other than what they might have stated.

You've also probably heard people complaining that they were not selected for a role they coveted, saying that the selection was based on favoritism rather than merit.

And you've no doubt heard things like, "The CEO is just trying to increase earnings to pump up the value of his equity compensation; that's why our project didn't get funded."

Those comments may have been accurate. But they may also have no basis in fact.

If you want people to be engaged, they must trust the people around them, especially their leaders. The first building block of trust is transparency.

In the 1980s, there was a cultural shift in corporate America. One of the most influential organizations in that shift was Hewlett-Packard, or HP as it was affectionately referred to. HP applied the management systems championed by Edwards Deming, who had been part of the team sent to Japan after World War II, to help that country rebuild. Deming's ideas were re-imported to the U.S. when it was clear his methods were creating a dramatic resurgence of Japanese industrialization, to the point that better products were coming out of Japan than those made in the U.S. Toyota, an enthusiastic student of Deming's methods, soon overtook U.S. car manufacturers in quality and value.

Deming applied some simple methods, which were revolutionary at the time. Up until that point, most companies were still using management principles that were from the early days of the Industrial Revolution, reinforced by wartime "command and control" structures. In that culture, information was power, not to be trusted in the minds of employees who represented the cogs within the machinery of business.

Deming turned that over. He said that with information, more people would be able to make a positive impact on the critical performance measures of a business, because they had direct experience with what goes right and what goes wrong, which the leaders can't understand from the top floor of the building. He instituted such concepts as "quality circles" where the people doing the work joined together to find solutions to improve the quality of the products being made.

Following Deming's principles resulted in Japanese manufacturers rising out of their reputation as producers of cheap, low-quality products to being the world standard of quality and value. Toyota's rise through the 1980s forward is a direct result of applying Deming's methods and improving upon them over many years.

Then came Jack Stack and his turnaround of Springfield Remanufacturing Company. Jack was asked to take on a struggling business unit of International Harvester. The company was bleeding cash and was going to be shut down if Jack couldn't figure out how to save it. He had no direct experience with the business and its operations. So, he did something that no one had really done to that point. He shared all the information and asked the plant's employees—all of them—what could be done.

The success of that company is legendary. Jack wrote a book about his experience, "The Great Game of Business". That was the launch of the "open book" management philosophy.

Many companies have adopted these ideas to this point, but not as many as you would think. And even those that do share the business information and invite everyone to offer solutions may still hold some information back, or not reveal the real reasons why decisions are made. It takes a servant leader to go the rest of the way to be vulnerable by sharing every relevant piece of information.

I want to note here, before I go further on this subject, that there are legitimate reasons to not share everything all the time. Publicly held companies have regulatory constraints that must be adhered to, in terms of how it protects information so that it cannot be used by unscrupulous investors who want to trade on the private information, including insiders. Certain types of information must be disclosed formally as well, at prescribed points in time, to satisfy laws applying to public companies. And there's the need to protect the privacy of individuals, such as in maintaining confidence about employment related actions. Data privacy in general has swept around the world with a raft of regulatory frameworks implemented to ensure personal privacy is maintained. Intellectual property and proprietary information that are critical to a business' success must be protected from disclosure to competitors.

Even with those caveats, there is so much more that can be shared with everyone, to increase not only trust, but to dramatically increase the ability of everyone to contribute.

Here comes another Garry Ridge quote: "People who share the same facts, the same values and the same goals will likely agree on what needs to be done."

And here's a quote, humbly offered as my own: "In the absence of facts, people will assume the worst possible interpretation." Humans do this because we are neurologically "wired" to detect threats far more than we are prone to detect non-threats. This makes sense evolutionarily. In our roughly 350,000 years of known existence as the modern species of humans, all but about 10,000 years were spent in hunter-gatherer tribes of 150 people or less, where every day was an existential challenge. The people who weren't good at threat detection didn't last long enough to procreate.

To improve alignment and cohesive effort, and to prevent negative interpretations of any given situation or topic, it is therefore imperative to freely share the important information of the business. This includes the key metrics of business performance (yes, including profitability). But it also includes other kinds of information.

For example, a specific strategy may have been adopted by the company's leaders, but it isn't communicated throughout the organization. Or a decision about whether to invest capital equipment may have been made, but not advertised to those affected. Hiding (or simply failing to remember it's important to communicate) such decisions will hamstring your organization. It's like asking someone to run a race for you on one foot.

Other information types are also critical. I'll address compensation in the next chapter, but here's a preview: If people don't trust that decisions about their compensation have logic and fairness as the foundation, and are based on the principles of a meritocracy, they will only engage so much. They will not consider the whole company as part of their trusted circle. They will distrust leadership decisions about many things, if they don't trust decisions about pay, about promotions and about experiential opportunities.

Finally, as a leader, you must be transparent about your own personal goals and objectives, to be trusted by others. You must be open about your "learning moments". You must be seen accepting accountability for missed targets in areas of your responsibility, rather than deflecting it to others. You must be seen as the first to praise others for your successes, not grab the limelight for yourself.

"But if I am that transparent, sharing most of the information of the business, how decisions are made and my own personal objectives, then what authority and influence do I really have?", laments the command-and-control type manager.

What I have seen, with my own eyes over a period of over a half century of working for a living and also as a business owner, is that the servant leader amplifies success through others by behaving in this way, far beyond what that leader could achieve by sequestering information and hiding decisions. Edwards Deming showed this. Hewlett and Packard demonstrated it. Jack Stack proved it. So have I. So has Garry Ridge. There are many examples.

A year or so ago I was on a call with two founders of a rapidly growing food product company. Their market success was significant, and they realized they were on the road to realizing their vision. They were interested in talking to me about how to intentionally create an enduring, highly engaged organization and admitted they didn't have all the answers yet.

I asked the question I normally do of business owners when I'm just getting to know them. I asked, "What do you both want from your journey with your company? What do you hope to achieve personally in the next ten years?" The planning horizon of high engagement is no less than a decade.

One of the founders replied, "We'd like to achieve doubling our revenue in three years and sell to either a strategic buyer or private equity at 10-12 times EBITDA."

I replied, "Well, you can still implement the right actions to increase engagement, with a longer-term time horizon, as long as you are open with your employees about your individual objectives to cash out in three years."

That comment stopped them in their tracks. They did not feel comfortable sharing that information with their employees.

They thought they could do things to increase engagement in a year or two and then sell their business, leaving with a nice pay day and freedom to choose their next adventures. They thought high engagement was a competitive advantage that would bring them a higher multiple on exit. They didn't see engagement itself as the objective.

If a company's leaders are talking long-term thinking and "building for the future" with high engagement as a goal, but their actions are near-term focused and incongruous with words like "enduring", "sustainable" and "long-term vision", the hypocrisy will be visible to the company's employees. Hypocrisy kills positive, engaged cultures. It's okay to have a short time horizon and people will still be engaged, if they know the truth—and are going to participate in the rewards that might come with a "liquidity event".

So why don't more CEOs consciously adopt transparency across the range of business information, decision-making and organizational aspirations? One possible answer is that it takes intentional structure and effort to implement. I'll offer the concept of the "cascade".

One of the services I provided to WD-40 Company in my advisory work prior to joining the organization as a tribe member was to facilitate the three Global Leadership Council meetings scheduled during the fiscal year, which included senior leaders from around the world.

Each meeting had a strong agenda that covered the predictable topics of company performance, strategic direction, business challenges, organizational structure evolution, cross-regional programs and projects, etc. These meetings also had an educational component. Garry wanted to take advantage of having a lot of the company's leaders in one place, to provide an opportunity for growing collective skills and abilities.

As facilitator, my job was to help the group navigate the agenda effectively and efficiently, make sure everyone was heard and to capture the content of the meeting's results. I used PowerPoint to do so in real time, pausing the discussion occasionally to ask the group if what I had written was accurate and complete. By the end of the two or three days of meetings, we had a compiled, accurate set of information about what went on, what decisions were made, what next steps were, who was going to do those steps, etc.

That deck was then distributed to every leader who attended. When they returned to their home office, in whatever country they worked, they used that same deck to provide a briefing to their teams, who then did the same to their teams. As feedback was given or questions raised, those leaders answered them. If they couldn't, then the information flow went back up the leadership chain until it reached someone who could answer or respond to the feedback. Often, that two-way information flow resulted in new ideas being generated that modified the conclusions reached at the Global Leadership Council meeting. That was not only okay, but it was also expected, hoped for.

The "cascade" process took attention and discipline, but it didn't take any more time, because the leaders who attended the meeting had regular meetings with their teams anyway. And since the "minutes" of the meeting were taken real time, and validated in the moment, there was no lag between the meeting's end and the creation of the document that captured the work done. There was no time lost on the calendar awaiting edits and comments on the "minutes" of the meeting, which would have taken literally weeks. Actions agreed to at the meeting were therefore commenced in far less time than what would have otherwise been possible. And we had a record for the next meeting to see what we committed to accomplishing compared to what was achieved.

You may find other ways to accomplish such transparency and broad involvement in your business. Perhaps this idea will help. There are many good books written on the subject.

For a few decades now "open book" management has been a topic of much discussion. In its least radical form, it might be equivalent to sharing sales figures with clerical support employees who don't normally have access to that information. The other end of the spectrum would be giving employees complete access to all company information, like revenue, profit, shareholder distributions and...sometimes even individual salaries.

Now as soon as you start talking with people about the subject of sharing compensation information, all sorts of strong opinions surface. "That might work for a small company, but it's just not practical in an organization of thousands, or even hundreds." Presumably the objection here is that such information can be dangerous, if held in the "wrong" hands, in the "wrong" size company. Supposedly, there's an inherent human factor associated with size that prevents people from understanding and applying the information productively.

Another argument is: "If Frank has no day-to-day interaction with people in the shipping department, why should he have an opinion of what the shipping staff compensation is? How can that help Frank be more successful in his own department?" Here the logic is that daily interaction has an impact on whether Frank applies that compensation information productively.

Here's another common view: "People will spend all their time talking about how unfair the compensation differences are. We just don't need that kind of distraction." This perspective means leaders don't think they can successfully explain and justify compensation decisions in a way that employees will understand or accept as fair. The premise is that employees aren't smart enough to appreciate the rationale for the individual compensation differences. Or the fear is that employees will discover dumb or self-serving decisions that will cause embarrassment.

If any of these assumptions is valid, it indicates that the organization has some serious deficits, compared to what *could* be achieved with a stronger, transparent strategy of compensation disclosure. For example, if it's true that employees aren't smart enough to appreciate the rationale for making business-based compensation decisions, then it means they aren't smart enough to understand how a company makes money, enabling it to support its employees who have decided to earn their living in its employ. Imagine what you could accomplish if your staff *was* capable of understanding this. The "open book" experiment is to first educate people, release the information, then build on a team of business thinkers rather than sheep. The next chapter is focused on compensation, to go deeper into how and why to be transparent about pay.

But most possessors of the information aren't willing to let the cats out of the bags. With all the talk and publicity about "open book", it rarely goes so far in an organization that profits, let alone compensation data, are shared. I wondered for years why that would be. In my experience as a person whose desk has stopped bucks for some time now, the profits I've enjoyed were *because* of an open book approach, not despite it. The rare occasions where I've seen it in operation in other companies, I've noticed that they seem to do better in comparison to others. And they have a better time doing it.

It's not just me arriving at this conclusion. The Beyster Institute and the Kaufman Foundation are two very large, well-known non-profit organizations who promote many of these philosophies, starting primarily with sharing ownership with employees. These organizations were founded by phenomenally successful business builders who applied their theories personally and quite profitably.

"Open book" management principles go hand-in-hand with inviting employees to be shareholders and/or to act like owners. The Beyster Institute and the Kaufman Foundation have completed extensive research on equity sharing over the years. The last study I saw showed that companies who shared ownership and included employees in knowledge about the business outperformed their peers by as much as 35%, over time. And the quality of life in these kinds of organizations is usually quite a bit better: less fear, more initiative, higher productivity, more fun.

So, in my opinion, the presumptions and assumptions about the problems anticipated with an "open book" philosophy stem from fear: fear of not being able to control how information is used; fear of not being competent in leading without being a decider of who gets to know the facts of the business; fear of not being able to justify the way decisions are made because they are not logical or fair; fear of revealing information that would make people question how much the owners or senior leaders are taking out of the business; fear of people demanding more pay because someone else may be in a higher pay grade whom they think is either the same value or less than they are, etc. Until leaders face these fears the value of the "open book" will remain closed, the treasures within it unrealized.

At WD-40 Company we strived for transparency and truth, which is the foundation for trust in any relationship. Transparency and truth are also necessary ingredients for effective business leadership, achieving objectives, helping people grow in their abilities, squeezing all the learning out of our experiences...the list goes on and on.

Even with all your efforts to share information, to be open about objectives and motives, some people will still wonder what you're *really* thinking. They will suspect other motives exist. They will try to guess who you favor for an open position. They will look for clues about your true thoughts, suspecting that you haven't revealed everything. That's human nature. Don't get despondent when it happens, don't get angry that all your hard work to be transparent didn't convince them of your authenticity. That would be the frustrated parent, or the disappointed child talking. Stay "adult" and just continue to ensure you are behaving and communicating with honesty and transparency, congruent of word and deed. Most people in your organization will respond in kind.

COMPENSATION: WHERE CULTURE MEETS THE ROAD

The compensation philosophy and strategy of a company is one of the most important business factors affecting commercial success as well as human engagement. Compensation is usually at least half of the expenses of a business, after cost of goods, for product-based companies. For service companies, it can be 70-75%. Many organizations I've encountered fail to realize how intentional they must be about compensation, to create a viable, sustainable business, which is essential to creating a greater sense of engagement by the people working in their organization.

Compensation is one of the most important places that an organization's values are exhibited. Or not. Any discrepancy between the values and how people experience compensation personally is a wedge of hypocrisy that can seriously damage your company's human fabric of cohesion and engagement. How raises are determined, who is promoted (especially into leadership roles), and how rewards are shared will send a much more powerful message than any set of fine sounding words framed on a wall.

The first step in creating a conscious philosophy and strategy is getting the best data possible about the market for the talent that your business needs. You wouldn't contract with a supplier without obtaining market information about price and performance of your needed materials or services, would you? You'd get as much information as you could because you realize that negotiating properly with suppliers is a critical element of growing a profitable business. Building a market-based foundation of compensation is not only more likely to be accepted as fair by your employees, but also the most logical business approach to determining how to allocate your finite funds.

There are multiple credible sources for labor market data, including public information that can provide a valuable view of the general economy and cost of talent, across a wide spectrum of role types. More specific information within a career progression of a job type is usually purchased from commercial compensation survey companies, many of which specialize in certain industries or career fields. The reason you can't get it directly from other employers (or at least you shouldn't) is that doing so would be a violation of anti-trust laws that prohibit price-fixing in any free market.

There are a lot of compensation data sources that are not credible these days. Self-reported data by individuals is famously inaccurate. You must be careful that your data sources use validated methods of ensuring the information is as accurate as it can get, from primary sources, i.e., company records. Commercial survey companies get the data directly from their participating subscribers who are employers, as well as from publicly disclosed information that publicly listed companies must provide for certain executive positions. Trade associations sometimes provide collective data within an industry, partnering with an external compensation service firm to work with the association members. And government statistics which are readily available in various forms can be another tool to add to other, more directly derived sources.

But before you can seek out the labor market data from credible sources, you must define the roles sufficiently to be able to match your positions to those included in the compensation survey provider you employ. That detailed job profile, or job description as it has humbly been called for decades, is foundational yet again.

Translating the labor market information, properly matched to the roles in your company, to a market range of likely compensation is not that complicated but does take some judgment. As many compensation experts will tell you, it's a fair bit of science with a dash of art, based on experiential knowledge gained over years of studying labor market trends across many types of jobs.

Let's assume you've done that work and you now have a good idea of the range of compensation for each role in your company, in the current labor market within which you compete for talent. Now you must decide how to use the data to make decisions. What is your philosophy of compensation? What is your strategy?

For many years, business leaders have often taken the position that their company is only interested in hiring "A" players, and therefore offer compensation that would place incumbents at the higher end of the market ranges. You might see a statement like this: "We believe that we must attract and retain the best people. Therefore, we will maintain our compensation position at the 75th percentile of the market for each role." That is indeed a philosophy and strategy.

But it's a flawed strategy, from a business standpoint. If you take that position the actual rates paid will accelerate ahead of other employers who don't similarly target the same percentile, which will cause you to adjust pay at a higher rate than the overall market, further up the range to maintain your 75th percentile position. If you do that for several years, there will eventually be a downturn in the general economy, or perhaps just in your industry or just your company, when revenue slides. Even if all the people you hired were indeed phenomenal, i.e., all "A" players, there are powerful external forces in the economy that can swamp any company's star team. When the Great Recession hit in 2008-2009, only a tiny fraction of employers was unaffected. And if *all* your competitors followed the same aggressive strategy in a given year, the median range of actual rates paid would simply be what used to represent the 75th percentile.

When the inevitable downturn hits, such a company's cost structure is differentially elevated compared to its competitors who may not have universally followed the same philosophy. Now your company is at a disadvantage in the market compared to competitors who didn't follow your aggressive market positioning, and you have limited ability to adjust product or service pricing to match the increased competition for reduced demand, and still retain the outstanding performers you hired. If all competitors followed your aggressive compensation strategy and chased the labor market median quickly higher, the first companies who eliminate labor and its cost will gain a pricing advantage.

For companies who accelerated their fixed labor costs beyond the moderate position of their labor markets, the only response possible in a significant downturn is to let some, maybe a lot, of those great people go out the door. These are people you hired because they were the best, right? You put a lot of time and money into keeping them, rewarding them. You developed them and spent years building effective relationships. Now you watch all that investment walk out, at your behest. You're not just losing the prior investments, either. You're also losing all future contributions those people would have made to your business.

Lots of companies, whole industries even, accept this cycle calmly. The aerospace industry is not built around stability of its labor force; that industry famously hires and fires as orders come and go. If you ask people who work in that industry how they feel about it, many are resigned to the cycles and don't really allow themselves to identify too closely with any one employer. They see themselves as members of an industry, shopped out to specific companies as fortunes change. They don't "dig in" and commit fully to any employer because they know their employer is not committed fully to them. No wonder aerospace contractors working with the government seem to always run over budget and miss the deadlines.

Other industries similarly view their people as a variable cost, to be grown or shrunk according to near-term financial conditions. While shareholders may applaud such cost-cutting and reward the public companies who do layoffs with a higher stock price, the longer-term prospects for success of those companies are diminished from what they could have been with a different approach to how people are viewed and paid.

As of the writing of this book, we are seeing technology companies laying off tens of thousands of people, many of whom they hired at a high premium during the unexpected steep rise of demand in the first two years of the pandemic. These companies, like Amazon, Meta, Alphabet and Twitter, chased the revenue, bribing people in a tight labor market with ever higher compensation. A short time later, they are shedding humans as fast as they can to protect their profitability and their stock price. For many people who entered their careers in these companies in the last ten years, this is the first time they have experienced such massive downsizing. The attractive cultural fabric that high-flying technology companies built, and with it their ability to attract great talent, lays on the cutting room floor.

The key point I want to make here is that if your compensation philosophy and strategy is not built to protect your employees' livelihoods in hard times, you cannot expect people to think long-term about their roles, let alone their careers, committing fully to the organization for years to come. The first time they experience a layoff environment in your business, even if they are not one of those let go, their psychological connection to the company and therefore their level of engagement will be significantly eroded, if not completely dissolved.

In the 70-year history of WD-40 Company, as I write this, there has never been a layoff due to a business downturn that forced reductions in labor costs at any of the company's global locations. Even through multiple recessions, including the Great Recession and the COVID pandemic. In the first year of the Great Recession, and at the outset of the pandemic in 2020, the only action taken was a one-year freeze on base salaries. There were no layoffs, no pay cuts, no loss of benefits. Even the discretionary portion of the company's 401(k) profit-sharing contribution to employee retirement accounts continued. How could the company afford to retain all employees in these calamities, and keep their compensation whole?

In 2002, Garry and his senior leaders in finance and HR asked me to help them redesign their compensation philosophy and strategy. Up to that point, the company had followed the practice stated above of aiming for base compensation at the 75th percentile of the market. They didn't have broad market data, so the positioning was essentially a guess, but accelerated fixed labor costs was the result. The data wasn't collected in the U.S. let alone globally, in any methodical process. The company paid discretionary bonuses not tied to performance. In fact, whether profits went up or down, the bonuses were routinely provided. This dynamic caused a strong sense of entitlement in the employee population; the culture was not that of a performance-based meritocracy.

This is a good place to mention that you can achieve a high engagement score for the wrong reasons. If you treat people like children, behaving as an overly protective parent, providing base compensation and benefits at the high end of the market and bonuses disconnected from performance, you will attract and retain people who like to be taken care of. They will report high satisfaction—as long as the gravy train continues. Garry knew that he wanted to change the culture, to create an organization comprised of conscious, accountable adults who joined together to achieve amazing things, sharing in the results as equal participants in the great game of business.

The first step, of course, was getting market information, beginning with the U.S. and Canada, where most employees worked at that time (that ratio has since shifted as the company successfully implemented its global growth strategies; there are now more employees outside of the U.S. and Canada).

The next step was changing the market positioning philosophy. The new market position was to set the company targeted total base compensation, in *aggregate*, to match the median of the labor markets applicable. This meant that when people were hired, they were offered compensation according to their ability to contribute, targeting the median. It should be noted that it took three years of applying this approach to realize the goal of having aggregate base salaries aligned with the median of the labor market ranges.

Concurrent with the second step above, the discretionary bonus methodology was scrapped. In its place we designed a performance-based incentive that was pegged to growth in profit year over year. Each year, after profit was calculated, the next year's targets for minimum and maximum incentive payout were set according to growth levels that accomplished the following objectives:

- Profit growth to provide acceptable returns to stockholders who valued long-term investing
- Profit growth to provide operating and investment capital for the business
- Profit growth to reduce or eliminate reliance on debt
- Profit growth to pay taxes
- Profit growth to fund incentive payouts to people

With steady, moderate growth in revenue and profit, people could earn a significant amount of incentive compensation. The incentive level for each role was chosen to be, at maximum, two times the median value of short-term incentives (STI) for the role in the relevant labor market. "Relevant labor market" was defined as the country within which the person resided.

While the overall position of all base compensation for the company was maintained at the median, because of the profit-based incentive design people could earn at or above the maximum *total* cash compensation range for their position, in their market, when performance was strong. Leadership's commitment was to establish strategies and plans that could achieve at least half of the maximum, which would put the company at the market median overall for total compensation.

Incentive payouts have generally averaged around 60% of maximum over a period of many years, which is above the markets' median STI payouts. Some years have been at the high end, some have been below the targeted 50% payout. It takes a strong business strategy and sound commercial leadership to achieve this kind of historical average payout, of course.

An early decision was to include everyone in the incentive compensation plan, even if the role wasn't customarily provided such incentives in other companies. The ratio of base pay that the incentives represented was set at no less than 10%, until the role in question reached a market level that did usually receive such an incentive, which was then calculated based on two times the median for the role in each market. By this intentional design, every employee in the company had the same type of cash base and incentive as the CEO or other executives, based on the same metrics. And the incentives paid for themselves, which meant that after the necessary uses of profit were satisfied, the additional profit paid for the incentives.

Therefore, a major reason why WD-40 Company has not had to resort to cost-cutting layoffs, even in the Great Recession or the pandemic disruptions that are still reverberating as of 2023, is that the fixed compensation structure in the company stays at a manageable level, even when revenue may drop significantly. By leveraging more of the total compensation "pie" into the variable, profit-based performance-based segment of incentives, the business model has a structural financial shock absorber to protect the business, its stockholders and the people who earn their livelihood within the company.

This strategy works for both public and private companies. I employed the same methodology in my consulting business long before I met WD-40 Company. It allowed us to weather a decline in revenues of as much as 30%, without having to impact compensation. We could withstand a 40% drop in revenue before having to face the prospect of a layoff. We never got close to that point, even during two recessions.

WD-40 Company, and other companies I've founded, based cash incentives on the profitability of the organization. In most cases, I've advised the same for my clients. This is a team-centered approach and aligns the economic interests of the organization's people with those of shareholders. Pre-revenue (and thus pre-profit) startups are an exception, where the majority of incentive is typically in the form of equity, aiming for a "liquidity event" (going public or being acquired). But eventually, every for-profit enterprise will need to generate profits to continue, let alone grow.

I've talked with leaders who feel that this collective design to achieving incentive payouts can reward slackers and underpay "star" performers. They say that individual incentives are more motivating because the achievement of individual objectives is within the control of the person who is attempting to earn the incentive.

My response, based on experience, is that very few people can achieve their objectives entirely on their own. And even if they did, individual objective-based incentives can result in paying out significant amounts even as the company performs poorly overall. I believe business is a team sport. If someone isn't carrying their portion of the load, it's leadership's accountability to know that and address it soon.

With the history of success in earning payouts at WD-40 Company and protecting people in hard times from the specter of losing their livelihood, engagement has blossomed. Again, a person can't think about long-term commitment and contributing over many years if, like at Twitter in 2022-2023, they must constantly be worrying about getting a termination text or email.

Refinements of the basic incentive structure implemented at WD-40 Company in 2002-2003 were made as time went on. The apportionment of incentives was allocated according to performance by country, then stretch target or wider team, then by global performance. Enhancements in equity compensation for long-term incentives of specific roles were made. Those long-term incentives were applied to roles that had multi-year impact on the business and for which such compensation was a broad market practice.

When I joined the company formally in 2012, we implemented a new global compensation data provider (Korn Ferry's "Hay" system) so that the same methodology could be applied across countries where types of roles, career progressions and titling differed greatly. The compensation system has been built steadily on the founding principles, refining the market analyses, and continuing the effort to properly value each role within a given labor market.

A final design element that is important to share with you is that each salary range was divided into three segments. The middle segment represents the center of the distribution curve of rates paid in the market. This middle section is about two thirds of the population of a given market range, and logically represents the incumbents in the role who can fulfill most, if not all, of the functional requirements of the position. Below that "zone" is the first segment, where people are paid if they are relatively new to the role and have not yet demonstrated full competence. The higher segment is where people are paid because of achieving truly advanced competency, making them more valuable as compared to others with less experience and ability to contribute. "Advanced" incumbents are typically starting to contribute at the next higher position in the career progression or are fulfilling additional functional responsibilities outside of their current role.

When people were offered a role at WD-40 Company, the candidate evaluation process (which is content valid and based on demonstrations of behavioral evidence of competency as well as character and cultural "fit") revealed where in the salary range the new person should be paid. Most people will fall in the "fully competent" middle section of the range. It is a good thing, however, to hire people who are not yet fully competent, as stated earlier in this book, providing they have the aptitude and motivation to advance in their abilities at a good pace. They are more engaged and excited about the role. This has the added benefit of moderating fixed labor costs to the left of the median of the market, and offsets the occasional need to hire a person with truly advanced competencies at the higher segment of their market range. Coupled with the philosophy that leaders are teachers who are accountable for assisting people to grow in their abilities, this compensation system and bias to hiring people who are motivated with high aptitude, but not yet fully competent, results in higher performance over a longer period, with higher engagement, at a more conservative fixed cost.

The competency-based placement in a range is also addressed in the ongoing performance leadership dialogue that occurs between coaches and tribe members quarterly. The discussion includes which competencies a person needs to develop, which have been mastered and which competencies displayed are above expectations, or "advanced".

The properly defined job description therefore contains the foundational information needed for 1) labor market compensation analysis, 2) establishing the competency requirements to be successful, and 3) the basis for development planning and providing experiences that will accelerate the individual's capabilities. Gaining the skills and knowledge to know how to evaluate competencies and contributions, and thus how to help people develop over time, takes conscious effort and disciplined application of the principles described. You may be thinking, "Not many people can do that." If you believe this, then you would likely think that it's not possible to develop strong leaders, if "strong" means they can operate these methods and create a fair meritocracy where people know what they need to do to demonstrate competencies and leaders know how to help them grow. I've seen that most leaders are quite capable of applying these principles, given some education and coaching, and are motivated to apply them.

Returning now to the subject of transparency and trust.

At WD-40 Company we embarked on a journey to apply the "open book" approach to compensation. It took a few years to complete the educational process once we had the global compensation structure and system in place. We started first with leaders, so that they could independently answer compensation questions without needing to refer people to HR. Leaders need to own that subject and be able to discuss the philosophy as well as the methods. If your own leader cannot explain how compensation decisions are made, how confident are you that your livelihood is being cared for in capable hands?

We also found mistakes in how people were being paid. Wherever there was a case that a person was placed lower in the relevant range than their demonstrated competency, or if they were paid below the minimum of the adopted market ranges, they received corrective adjustments.

Once the corrections were made and education completed, we then provided full access to every person within a country to view the important information, which included all position descriptions in that country or region, as well as the salary ranges applicable to each role. Now employees had the information they needed to evaluate their career path, to pursue their aspirations. Coupled with the principle that people should be treated as accountable adults, responsible for their own choices, compensation transparency greatly enhances that adult mind state.

While some of the leaders were a bit nervous just before we opened the "book", the result was a strongly positive reaction by employees. We only had a few questions from people and those were answered quickly, with understanding and acceptance.

There are some countries where this "open book" method was not applied, but work continued to develop the right approach to extending the transparency of compensation to cultural environments where this philosophy is considered a radical departure from convention and custom. I have been told by current leadership that this journey of compensation transparency is continuing.

To conclude this topic, here is a summary of the design elements described in this chapter and their impact on enhancing engagement:

- A compensation structure of moderated fixed costs and strong variable incentives that protects the business performance and the livelihoods of the people within it, and thus at the same time creates psychological safety.

- This security of livelihood allows a person to think longer-term, committing more of their mental energy to their role and their sense of opportunity. They are more engaged.

- Sharing strong incentives with everyone for achieving profitable performance, which aligns behavior and rewards for results, for all stakeholders, as a team. Shared rewards, using the same metrics for all recipients from the CEO down, creates cultural "glue" and motivational alignment.

- Transparency of the compensation system elements and how decisions are made, which increases trust and confidence that people will be fairly treated. Trust is elevated. Again, higher engagement results.

- Transparency of the roles and associated compensation ranges, which gives people the information they need to make their own decisions about their future aspirations, including knowing what is required to earn advancement. Autonomy is a key inherent motivator, which increases engagement. People behave as accountable adults, making their own life decisions with the information and tools needed.

- Basing compensation and advancement on demonstrated competencies and contributions, which creates a meritocracy where anyone, from any background or demographic segment, can achieve their goals through their own merit. People therefore feel like they belong, increasing engagement.

Your compensation strategy and methodology reflect your culture, your values, and your leadership philosophy more accurately than anything you might otherwise say. It is an emotional and potent factor in everyone's life. It truly is where culture meets the road.

My litmus test of compensation practices is whether I would be proud to describe exactly how decisions are made about people's money, to the entire company. If I wouldn't, then the practices are probably sketchy, not logical, relationship-based rather than merit-based, applied disparately or approached like individual negotiations. If I *would* be proud, then there's no reason not to open the kimono and be transparent.

CONSTRUCTIVE CONFLICT RESOLUTION

One of the most popular and useful courses taught in the Leadership Laboratory at WD-40 Company was how to resolve conflicts constructively and positively. Throughout my working life, I've seen the continuing damage that is done within organizations due to the friction of conflict. If the principles of effective conflict resolution are taught, the friction diminishes significantly.

When I or my fellow faculty in the Leadership Lab began this workshop, we would often start with a disclaimer: "If I really knew how to constructively resolve conflicts, I'd be working for the State department or the U.N., solving the boiling cauldron of the Middle East, the war in Ukraine or relations with China."

Conflicts between people, let alone countries, are famously difficult to resolve. But with a desire to do so, willing participants in a conflict can and do find the path to a peaceful, constructive resolution. And that's the key; there must be at least one of the parties willing to start taking the necessary steps to find a peaceful solution. The actual steps to achieve this are available; that's not the problem. The desire to achieve constructive resolution is the missing ingredient in most enduring conflicts.

If the culture you are building is sufficiently positive, where most people do feel like they belong, people care about each other, and the values are supportive of constructive conflict resolution, the odds go up that teaching the techniques will result in less unresolved conflict.

The first principle of conflict resolution is to recognize that when allowed to simmer without resolution, most conflicts don't go away. They can burn under the surface for literally years, then flare up at inopportune moments when people are least prepared to address them, usually in conditions of high stress. All the unresolved conflicts in your organization act like sand in a transmission. You can't see the sand directly, but you feel the grind.

Teaching conflict resolution does a few things to counter the negative effects. One result is that talking about conflict becomes normal and natural, even beneficial in an organization. Some of the fear of the subject is taken away. It allows the objective, adult mind state to engage in the exploration. And it's not a ruse. Conflict *is* normal and often beneficial. That's how the best ideas are arrived at, for example, through debate of disparate viewpoints. People learn how to address disagreements quickly and respectfully. This accelerates progress towards achieving objectives.

Another benefit to teaching conflict resolution is that the more people who gain some skills in this important area, the more likely it is that they will have a common language and method to approach each other when the inevitable friction occurs. It's like having a can of WD-40® Multi-Use Product on your belt all the time, ready for that squeaky conflict.

Yet another benefit is that once a person acquires the information and methods of conflict resolution, they now can choose to act, reinforcing the mindset of the accountable adult. You, as a leader, will be less frequently asked to play judge and jury.

But what if you are the one causing the conflict? You may not even know that is the case. I can guarantee you that eventually you will be a source of conflict if you aren't already.

Included in our Leadership Lab coursework on conflict resolution is an exploration of the sources of conflict. If participants in a conflict can really peel down the layers to reveal the actual sources of the friction, the resolution necessary is much easier to identify. If a leader is helping other people resolve conflicts and is not a participant, the proper approach to mediating is as an enzyme, not a reagent. An enzyme potentiates chemical reactions between other compounds, without being changed or consumed in the process. A reagent is an active part of the reaction, and changes in the process. Acting as a catalyst means bringing conflicted parties together, stating the conflict, and then inviting them to work together to resolve it.

If as a leader you think you're an enzyme but discover that you are part of the reaction, now you get the chance to deal with your own part in the conflict. The way you respond to such a case will teach everyone around you how conflict is to be handled in your organization…or not.

If you get angry or withdraw from the interaction, applying the force of your authority to end the discussion, you may think you're stopping the conflict. "I made the decision and we're done!" you might think. Well, *you* might be "done", but the unresolved conflict, which lives and breathes in the minds and hearts of those involved, will carry on. They just won't come to you with it anymore. They'll work around you, hide things from you, become despondent or resigned. They'll disengage.

Addressing conflicts constructively that result from your own behavior, your decisions and your actions has a huge positive impact. People won't be afraid to come to you with constructive suggestions, counterpoints to your decisions or new ideas that are not aligned with the direction you chose. They will know that you will listen to understand, you'll be willing to learn new information and revisit prior directives if someone feels strongly enough about it to bring it to you for a discussion.

Garry's example of being firm of opinion then immediately questioning his own conclusion showed everyone else how to address conflicts in general, with a healthy dose of self-examination and being open to new ways of thinking.

In our Leadership Lab course on constructive conflict resolution, we taught the emotional dynamics that occur in the state of conflict, and how to recover an objective, rational, "adult" mind state. Non-physical confrontation is experienced neurologically and psychologically the same as physical confrontation. Our fight/flight/freeze response kicks in, to the degree of fear or anger associated with the subject of the conflict.

Much has been written about this threatened state of mind, which I won't repeat here. One neurological fact deserves highlighting, however. In the words of my Leadership Lab colleagues Joanne and Roxanne, "When emotions go up, intelligence goes down". We taught methods of regaining a calmer state of mind, to move from sympathetic nervous system enervation to that of parasympathetic activation. It is a lot about breathing, planning, practice, and repeated opportunities to directly address conflict, one-on-one. With such repeated positive experiences, the fear of conflict itself is much reduced over time and experience.

We also taught the four methods of resolving conflict positively, once the rational mind was ready and the source of conflict was identified, used singly or in combination:

Avoidance

This strategy is used when all the facts are not known, or the conflict will take care of itself, or one is not yet prepared to address the conflict objectively and calmly. Not used out of habit alone, because as I said unresolved conflicts don't go away; they instead get worse and erupt destructively, unpredictably.

Maintenance

This strategy is used to continue a *productive* conflict, such as debating disparate strategies, designs, or methods so that the best of the options will rise to the top. This is competition for the best outcome to benefit all.

Reduction

This is "giving in" to what someone else wants, because there is little or nothing to lose, and much to gain in demonstrating the ability to support someone else's objective or idea. Requires self-confidence and being unafraid to appear "weak". When it's done involuntarily, it feels like losing. When it's done voluntarily and strategically, it's brilliant. This creates goodwill and increases the chances of reciprocal behavior.

Engagement

This is focusing attention and energy to engage closely with the counter party, to find a third solution that can satisfy both parties' individual objectives without loss to either, even though the solution is not one of the two competing proposals or desires. This method has high potential for rewards but takes the most skill and equanimity to be successful. Therefore, it is often the least used, a powerful tool that gathers dust on the shop shelf.

The methods of applying these approaches are fairly simple in concept but take self-awareness, calmness and maturity to apply in complex situations. Our course gave people the opportunity to practice the skills in a safe setting. Our internal HR team provided individual coaching, rehearsal practice and support as needed.

There are other, various good models to choose from as well, with overlapping principles that may be described somewhat differently. I'd recommend you consider the National Conflict Resolution Center as a potential external advisory resource.

They are a well-respected, forty year old non-profit focused on all aspects of conflict resolution in organizations and can be a powerful additional partner.

Whatever tools or approaches you apply, as CEO, you must ensure that conflicts are not hidden, that they are addressed as quickly as is practical and productive, and that people feel respected in the process of constructive resolution. Especially if the source of the conflict is you. If you and your other leaders are successful, engagement will rise even in such situations, with people ever more capable of preventing the frictional damage of unresolved conflict.

BELONGING

Your shared values and purpose will attract like-minded people who will feel they belong, to a large extent. But belonging goes broader and deeper.

How do you know that you belong in a group or organization? What are the feelings which tell you that this is true?

When asked this question, most people who do feel they are in the right place respond with:

"I feel comfortable. I'm not anxious."

"I feel that I can be myself and act naturally."

"I don't feel like I have to change who I am to be accepted."

"I feel supported by others. I feel like they have my back, and I have theirs."

"I feel acknowledged and respected for the work I do."

"I don't feel dismissed or judged for who I am."

"I feel welcome wherever I am or whomever I'm with, in the organization."

"I enjoy being with my colleagues at work and while in social settings."

"I know that my leaders and my colleagues care about me as a person."

To create a place where this is the way most, if not all people feel in your company, you must first examine your own biases and judgments. Yet again, as CEO, you are the prime example that others will follow.

For example, do you think that tattoos are inappropriate for a work setting? Do you think that people who marry someone of the same biological gender are wrong to do so? Do you criticize people who buy cars from Europe or Asia instead of the U.S.?

Do you think that some ethnicities or genders are less capable than others, for certain roles? Do you think a degree from Harvard always indicates a superior candidate compared to someone who graduated from, say, San Diego State University? Do you think that everyone should wear dress slacks or dresses to work, even if they are on a video call? Do you dislike people who laugh a lot during the workday?

The unconscious biases a CEO and other leaders have can serve to first limit the variety of people who are invited to join your company, and secondly will communicate subtly to others who is "in" and who is "out", through your expression, gestures, tone, movement and a thousand subtle cues in how you communicate. Worse, if your biases are not job-related and are openly acted upon to make decisions about who to hire, who to promote, who gets recognition, etc., the messaging is massively impactful in communicating what characteristics and behaviors are welcomed and which aren't.

I am going to assume that if you decided to read this book, you have the goal of creating a culture of inclusion, a meritocracy where all are welcome if they are able and willing to contribute to the success of the organization, pursuing the career path of their choice, in a manner that is aligned with your values. What you may not realize is just how your biases which are not related to performance of a role can work against your objectives. Now amplify the negative effect by all the other leaders in your company who will emulate your biases and add their own.

We all have biases, which are built from beliefs, prior experiences, and even personal values. It is a difficult and important process to identify one's own biases and to decide whether they should be applied to make people decisions.

Let's take an example. Let's say you have an opening for a logistics manager. You get a good response of applicants. One of the candidates has significant experience directly related to your industry and the job's required competencies. This candidate, "Jill", marked "yes" on her application to the question of whether she was convicted of a felony, and there is a five-year gap in her employment.

What was your first internal reaction to this news? Was it to discount her candidacy? Would you automatically eliminate her from further consideration before you know the nature of the conviction?

Another example. At the company's holiday party, you notice that one of your senior managers, who is married, is spending a lot of time in close conversation with a single woman from another department. There's light touching and a lot of laughter as they both sip wine. What is your first thought as you imagine this scene? Do you think it's inappropriate? What if your senior manager is a married woman rather than a man? Less concern? The same? Or more?

Many factors can trigger biases. Skin color. Exotic surnames. Fashion choices. Backgrounds of education and specific experiences. Lapses in employment. Headwear. Accents. The kind of car a person is driving. Body art and piercings. Speech habits. How much attention someone seems to desire. The type of office decorations someone chooses to display. How messy their office is. The list is nearly endless. While some biases may have a valid basis in job-related experience and history of prior events, even those can be fallacious at times.

As CEO, you must examine your own biases and decide which are empirically valid in the context of your business (which means you can establish a direct connection between the bias and the impact on performance in a role or the success of the organization), and which are extraneous.

A bias I have is that the more inclusive you can be in not only tolerating human differences, but also in celebrating those differences, the more welcoming a culture you will create, where most if not all people feel they do belong. Everybody is a bit of a weirdo, in their own way, just like every family has a taste of unique dysfunctionality. Simply being tolerant of quirks is not the goal. The goal is discovering the unique gifts that those differences can contribute to the organization.

My bias is built on my values, but also on decades of evidence from my own companies and experiences that my bias is valid in the creation of engaged, high-performing organizations. And many research studies report that cohesive diversity in an organization creates a differentially positive impact on performance. For example, McKinsey and Company has studied this over a number of years. In May of 2020, in their third report entitled "Diversity wins: How inclusion matters", McKinsey's study included over 1,000 large companies across 15 countries, with data collected in 2019 prior to the onset of the COVID-19 pandemic. McKinsey's longitudinal study began in 2014. The 2019 analysis found that companies in the top quartile for gender diversity on executive teams were 25 percent more likely to have above-average profitability than companies in the fourth quartile—up from 21 percent in 2017 and 15 percent in 2014. As relates to ethnic diversity, the top-quartile companies outperformed those in the fourth quartile by 36 percent in profitability, slightly up from 33 percent in 2017 and 35 percent in 2014.

Another bias I have is that it is important to file and clear email content daily. Others don't share my view. And I've noticed that they still perform quite well. Therefore, my bias is a personal decision and shouldn't be applied to how I lead others or evaluate their performance. So, I don't rely on this particular bias to make people decisions.

When I retired from WD-40 Company in 2021, there were about 600 tribe members residing in 16 countries, speaking at least eight languages, living in the full range of government types. Every color, size and shape of human was represented. Every gender and variation thereof. Most major religions were represented, even the absence of any religion. When we would have global meetings where representatives of each region collected, it was like being on the U.S.S. Enterprise from the Star Trek series. That which bound us together as a global tribe was far stronger than our differences. As I mentioned in the introduction, the culture of WD-40 Company was found around the world and it gave me hope that humans could really form bonds of mutual support and cohesion, no matter where on the planet they lived.

To achieve such inclusion is no small feat. Even if your biases are categorized and the irrelevant or destructive ones neutralized, you still need to demonstrate by your behavior, and the behavior of all your leaders, that you accept people for who they happen to be, without judgment about personal factors. The only judgment to apply is whether they are living your organization's values and contributing to the success of the company as needed in their role.

I'm not someone who subscribes to one spiritual organization or another, but I do take truths from where I find them. I remember the story of the Sermon on the Mount from when I was a child in catechism. I remember the story of Jesus saving the woman from being stoned to death, and the admonition to not be so quick to criticize others given we are all flawed. Those tales had a big impact on me. They said to me that a loving response was to judge no one and to go out of your way to help others in need, no matter who they were. That made sense to me. Similarly, Buddhism reveres all life, considering even the lowest form to be sacred. That made sense to me. The Pagan celebration of life made sense to me. I think kindness is the highest form of spiritual practice. Bringing non-judgment and kindness into your leadership approach will likely be the most important factor in creating an inclusive environment where everyone can feel like they belong.

But like the other elements discussed so far, kindness is necessary for a culture of belonging, yet insufficient. Active outreach to ensure qualified people from all backgrounds have an opportunity to earn the invitation to join the organization is also necessary. You can't create a multi-colored quilt of humans if you always pull on the same threads when you go looking for folks to join you.

I was talking with Trisha this morning. She is a very skilled human resources advisor. She described hiring someone recently who she said was her first "equity" hire. I asked what she meant.

Trisha said, "A candidate approached me personally, rather than applying online according to our advertised methodology. He explained that he couldn't afford digital tools like a laptop or smart phone, so was unable to apply as instructed. I realized that he was not alone. There are a lot of people who may be quite capable who are not able to have access to the modern digital world. This is the often-cited 'digital divide', between those who have technology and those who do not. I told him about the available equipment and tools at public libraries and made an exception to ensure he could apply. He's a great candidate and we have brought him on."

Reaching out to the broadest possible range of qualified applicants, getting creative on how you bring them into the process, will ensure that you truly are inclusive. Applying content-valid selection methods to focus on evaluating competencies, character and motivation will help eliminate extraneous biases. Then, once they are in the organization, continuing that inclusive meritocracy will cement the feeling of belonging for everyone. And your business will be stronger, more creative, more resourceful.

Another area to pay attention to is internal segregation. It's impossible to eliminate it, but you can remove the negative effects on how welcome people feel. By "internal segregation" I mean the categorization of people according to necessary factors that define groups, that divides the organization through boundaries of function, role, authority, project, product line, geography, etc.

For example, for many years at WD-40 Company we had a group of leaders called the Global Leadership Council, which was comprised of the CEO, his direct reports and the finance leaders of each trading bloc. That was a necessary segregation, practical and effective in forming aligned views of strategy and objectives. You can't effectively run a global company in 16 countries if everyone is invited to such planning and decision events. The role (not the person) determined inclusion or exclusion and that's not a bad thing. As I've said previously, decision-making in a business doesn't work as a democracy or through required consensus, at least in my experience.

But some segregation is done that isn't necessary and can erode the sense of inclusion that people feel. For example, a popular idea is that a company's leaders should identify who within the organization has high potential. The short-hand lingo is that they are "hi-po". As soon as you use that term within your organization, and begin to put names inside the definitional boundary, you are telling the rest of the people who are not included that they are not "hi-po"—they are "lo-po".

If we ignore the fact that most of the time senior leaders who claim they can spot "hi-po" individuals are wrong (they typically base their assessment on sparse interactions that comprise a small sample of the full set of behaviors of the subject), it is still destructive to form such cohorts who are subsequently treated like they are special. They get extra development opportunities. They go to special meetings or attend private educational experiences. Sometimes, they can start to slack off their efforts or ignore requests for help from others because they think they are headed for greater things. They can get cocky. This dynamic erodes the sense of engagement by others who can feel excluded, like they didn't get a chance to prove they were worthy of such valuable experiences.

Maintaining a meritocracy prevents this destructive segregation. If your philosophy is that everyone has high-potential and it's up to each person to demonstrate that fact by the contributions they make and their increasing capabilities, you don't need to form a special club. Everyone can earn the right to receive developmental opportunities, everyone can apply and will be selected based on demonstrated performance and the limits of your budget. Those that you don't select for development programs deserve to know why they were not selected, and how they could better prepare for future opportunities. Your reasons need to be job-related, factual, and based on observable evidence. If you apply this respectful, inclusive approach based on merit alone, most people will understand not only why they weren't selected for an opportunity, they will know what they must do to earn another.

By welcoming variety, celebrating differences, allowing people to be their authentic selves within the context of a meritocracy, living the values daily, your chances of creating a sense of belonging for the vast majority of the people in your organization go way up.

THE DARK SIDE OF HIGH ENGAGEMENT

What could be bad about very high engagement? "Bad" is a relative term, of course. I would much rather face the challenges that come with high engagement than accept the negative or even mediocre experience of being a part of an organization where engagement is very low. But there are some detrimental effects of high engagement that you, as CEO, will need to pay attention to, should you succeed in your efforts to create a sustainable, positive culture where people really dig in to contribute.

If over 90% of your organization's people continually contribute above and beyond what is expected, they will be working with focus, attention, diligence, and a deep desire to make a difference towards achieving the purpose of the company. They will willingly work long hours, take on extra assignments and sacrifice their own personal comfort to achieve great things. This can cause people to damage themselves in the pursuit of those goals. It's often called "burnout", and it can happen with the best of intentions.

I think there are two reasonable definitions of burnout. One is exhaustion, simply reaching the end of one's physical and mental abilities to continue to exert effort. If you've ever pushed your body beyond its abilities, you've experienced this. You can't get enough oxygen to the hard-working cells, creating the condition of hypoxia, using the body's own tissue for energy, literally eating oneself alive. Working long hours, not getting enough sleep, not enough exercise, taking care of the kids first– all these things create exhaustion.

Another definition of burnout that makes sense is chronic stress, when the sympathetic nervous system (the one that causes fight-flight-freeze responses in a condition of perceived threats) dominates for too long. Deadlines, urgent messages, last-minute requests, demands for response, long lists of action items and the uncertainty in which we all now live cause our sympathetic nervous system to run hot, all the time. Chronic stress is a well-known cause of many physiological problems.

The global events of the last few years have dramatically increased the demands on all of us, while at the same time increasing the perceived tenuousness of our futures. We're getting better at living through such times, if only because repetition of stimuli becomes attenuated in humans. We get used to a constant state, even if that constant state is ambiguity. But the toll on our minds and bodies is substantial. That's why people are making choices to change their lives, quit a toxic job, move to a new location, engage in a way of earning a living that is less stressful and find meaning in their work somewhere else. Couple these dynamics with a person's personal desire to give a lot to their beloved organization, and you have a recipe for self-inflicted damage.

Leaders have a direct impact on whether the conditions within their companies reduce burnout or increase it. I was talking with a senior vice president of an organization that generates $130 million in annual revenue. She was asking how she could improve the value and experience of the countless meetings that have become the norm during the pandemic, video call after video call after video call. I asked, "Do you really need all those meetings?" After a week or two of reflection, checking in with others, she found that she could cancel a significant number of the standing meetings and make others less frequent, thereby gifting her entire organization with the blessed luxury of time. Now they could devote more of their normal working day to producing results, rather than sitting in meetings discussing why the results hadn't yet been produced. Everyone was hugely relieved, and their stress diminished immediately. Their work hours went down while their performance went up.

I was talking with the COO of another company, who was bemoaning the fact that he was experiencing increased resistance to his directives and initiatives. He felt that people were becoming oppositional to what he believed were important actions that needed to be taken. I asked him, "How much of your work week is creating tangible results, versus meeting with others, setting direction, getting reports, making decisions and spending time thinking about the future?" He said, "In my role, I don't produce the results. My job is to lead."

"Exactly", I said. "You create work for others by calling meetings, asking for information, giving out assignments, sending emails that require responses, etc. What have you done lately to *reduce* the work loads of others, who are likely underwater and have been for a long time? When have you taken a task off the desk of one of your direct reports and done it yourself, to help them catch up?"

I had a mentor and boss early in my career who taught me this leadership lesson which has been one of the most important in my life. It was at a big aluminum factory, with 2,000 employees, 40 acres under roof. One day, he explained to me that an unexpected physical audit was necessary, to do an inventory of every product and all material in the entire plant. It had to be done by the next Monday, and today was Thursday. He said all the people in the "Head Shed" (non-production employees), including the General Manager of the plant, were going to help, which meant working through the weekend. I asked him why, and he said, "A leader shows they care about their people by sharing the same pain."

So, I said to the COO, "If you want to help your hard-working team not burn out, resign, become ill, etc., figure out how to reduce their work load, even if that means stepping in to do some of the actual work."

This is good advice in general. But in an organization of high engagement, you might get resistance when you try to help a person take better care of themselves. They don't want to admit their own limitations. They don't want to give up on the great work they are doing which is deeply meaningful to them. They don't want to forego exciting experiences that are in front of them. If you suggest that they take on fewer goals in the coming year, they might even argue with you. It's a delicate discussion to convince someone that they need to take on less. It could be perceived as a criticism of their abilities or your lack of confidence in them. But if you have truly established a trusting relationship with them as a coach and mentor, they will listen to you, because they will know that you care about them and their well-being.

I was so fortunate to work with an entire team of professionals at WD-40 Company who were highly engaged, ambitious and talented. My ongoing challenge was largely how to effectively moderate their enthusiasm for progress to achieve a pace that was healthy, sustainable, and which accomplished the right priorities for the business. As I told them one year, when we had achieved the construction of our global human resources functional design which was operating well, we needed to limit our new initiatives because each new functional capability came with an ongoing time commitment for operation and maintenance. It's exactly like a manufacturing plant. If you put in a new line, now you must run it, fix it when it breaks, keep up the preventive maintenance.

In my last few years as head of human resources for WD-40 Company, I became additional capacity for my team. When they were overflowing, I stepped in to help get things done, as another individual contributor working under their guidance. They were all quite capable people. They needed occasional coaching and a thought partner. They needed help when the volume of work put their nose under water.

A CEO can miss the signals of burnout from high engagement. You're not close enough to the actual work to know that it's happening. And people won't want to tell you that they are drowning. Unless you actively give people permission to say "no" when quality of work and their well-being are at risk, they will just try to please you and thus over commit. You need to ask people, "How are you? Is there anything I can do to make your work easier? Are there things I ask you to do that you are having trouble accomplishing because of workload?"

And you need to keep asking them. After a while, they may tell you the truth, when they believe you really want to know and will take action to help them. Your example will give other leaders permission and encouragement to do the same.

I've heard some CEOs say that setting dramatically ambitious objectives is how organizations make great progress, and I think that's often true. However, it takes wise and aware leadership to know when Big Hairy Audacious Goals, as Jim Collins phrased it, are inspiring—and when they're demoralizing. Just because people will enthusiastically attempt to go through a brick wall for you doesn't mean it's okay to keep asking them to when they are already bruised and battered.

Watch for the signs of "high engagement burnout". Some possible signs include:

- Increasing error rates across functional types (lots of little mistakes, big mistakes)
- Tempers getting shorter, increased interpersonal conflicts
- Increased absences due to illness or people continuing to work while they're sick
- Initiatives that come and go without formal completion or closure ("What ever happened to that marketing strategy we put in place three years ago?)
- Quality of work declines as number of tasks and projects are increasing
- People volunteering for extra assignments even if they are not meeting all their goals

Don't take high engagement for granted and assume that because people are willing to expend incredible energies, they are able to do so without significant personal damage. Help them throttle back if needed.

WHAT YOU SHOULD
EXPECT FROM HR

Half of my fifty-year career has been spent as an entrepreneur, having founded four businesses. A quarter has been as an internal HR professional and leader (which always came with other functional accountabilities like quality assurance, facilities, safety and ESG). A quarter has been in manufacturing, operations, and technical sales. So, I've been both a customer of HR, and a provider of HR services. This has greatly affected my view of what the function needs to contribute, and how.

My perspective of the HR role is primarily from the business leader's mindset because that is who I was, and those were my clients and business partners. From the viewpoint of the customer of HR services, I learned more about what the role could be, and should be, than I ever did while performing HR functional roles early in my career.

I had a unique opportunity while working at TRW in the 1980s, which crystallized my thoughts about how HR could best benefit the overall organization. I had joined TRW as Manager of HR for its printed circuit subsidiary in the Los Angeles area. Our leadership team worked well together. We were tasked with turning around a struggling business.

We succeeded. TRW decided to sell the business now that it was profitable, because it didn't really fit into the electronics segment strategy. Soon to be out of a job due to our success, I pursued opportunities elsewhere in the company. I got an interview with another larger TRW division in San Diego, LSI Products, which was making cutting edge (for that time) large scale integrated circuit devices. I was offered the job of leading recruitment and employee relations. About a year into that position, the semiconductor industry hit one of its cyclical troughs. Hiring wasn't necessary anymore. The general manager of LSI Products invited me to his office and offered me the job of running the back-end manufacturing group (taking the processed "wafers" of devices, making individual packaged components, testing, and shipping them to customers. This was an $80 million business annually, in late 1984. I would be leading a group of 120 people. I knew very little about how our highly technical, complex products were made.

People always felt the GM was "eccentric". Appointing me manager of back-end manufacturing proved it. To this day, I have no idea why he felt I could do the job. But I didn't want to be looking for work again, so I accepted the role gratefully. Over the next three years leading that group I learned a lot, such as that leading people isn't about telling them how to solve their challenges as much as it is about helping them get done what they already are committed to and capable of. My time as manufacturing manager at that facility was some of the most rewarding in my career. I think I can say that I earned their respect by the time my term was done.

When I walked down the hallway from HR to the manufacturing wing of the building, I passed through a curtain of perspective. My interactions with my former boss in HR changed instantly. I was, in my mind, a customer of HR services. That's how I approached my role while in that department, i.e., as a service provider to line leaders who were relying on me to help solve their talent needs and human conflicts.

But my former HR leader demonstrated that they did not view me as a customer. I got the message that people decisions were to be made by HR, not line or functional leaders. I escalated when I felt it important, but soon found that HR was allowed to operate with veto authority over leaders, and there didn't appear to be either a business case or a regulatory imperative that was foundational to HR's decisions.

Not all HR functions operate this way, but many still are allowed by their CEOs to take on more accountability for decisions than they should. I still encounter companies today that don't give hiring managers the authority to make job offers, even if they are within the strategy and philosophy of compensation decision-making the organization has adopted. HR functions are delegated the responsibility to inform people that they are being separated, when the decision is made by the functional leader of a group. HR is relied upon to decide when corrective performance counseling is required. HR is expected to lead "diversity, equity and inclusion" initiatives, without involvement by business leaders in other departments. These are not accountabilities that HR can or should fulfill in my view.

Well-meaning and dedicated HR professionals will accept the delegated responsibility with a desire to contribute to the business. But if they do, it will create a schism between leadership and the people being led. Employees will learn that the most sensitive elements of their personal experience within the organization are being handled by people to whom they don't report—compensation, performance counseling, exploring opportunities for advancement, educational opportunities, etc. And most of the time, HR practitioners don't understand the business well enough to make the right decisions about the people involved.

With this experience behind me, in 1989 when I formed HRG, Inc. as a service provider in human resources (along with other advisory services), I was intent upon being a valuable partner to line leaders. Our services were designed to improve the decisions that line leaders had to make. I didn't have to guess if our work was valued. I knew we were indeed of value because our clients paid our invoices and came back for more services. They referred other clients to us.

When I joined WD-40 Company to lead the global HR function, I brought with me that mentality and methodology of an advisor in human matters within a business. I found a talented group of HR professionals already within the company who were capable and open to this mindset. If you've ever taken on a leadership role where you "inherited" a team, you know that it doesn't always work out. But boy did I get lucky. I walked into a dream team.

With a customer service mentality, we became trusted advisors to leaders at WD-40 Company, helping them make their own decisions, supporting them as guides and experts in our various specialties of talent acquisition, compensation, regulatory compliance, benefits, employee relations, learning and development, organizational design and development.

We didn't make decisions 99.9% of the time. We routinely advertised that fact in all our interactions. Only in rare instances was it appropriate for any of us, me included, to use authority to settle a particular issue. And even then, we had a method of escalating disagreement between HR and a functional leader, which was advertised and welcomed. The pinnacle of that resolution process was the CEO.

Even the global HR principles and practices were not "owned" by HR at WD-40 Company. We offered recommendations, based on our expert opinion and experience, about how to standardize certain types of people decisions and methods. Those recommendations were presented periodically to the global leadership team to approve or not, or to modify, with ultimate decision rights held by Garry, our CEO. Therefore, the authority for the people practices, methods and decisions was never in the hands of HR.

I believe the CEO is the true, and indeed the only Chief Human Resources Officer in any organization. If the CEO, and by extension all the other leaders in the organization, do not take responsibility for decisions related to people practices, the employees in the company do not feel the trust and confidence in their leadership that is essential to creating high engagement. HR's job is to provide the information, tools, good counsel and support to improve the quality of decisions that others make. Not to act like line leaders.

We still hear a lot in the media about HR wanting a "seat at the table", meaning HR professionals don't feel invited or included in significant business matters or decisions. To achieve that "seat", many HR professionals think that usurping leadership authority over people decisions is the way they will succeed. Others in HR think that renaming the function will do the trick. "Human capital" still hangs on after its introduction over 20 years ago. Have you ever heard a more sterile, dehumanizing term for "people"? Recently I've noticed "People Operations" offered as a new term to presumably raise value of the role because the word "operations" sounds more centrally important in a business context. As Shakespeare taught us, "A rose by any other name..." is still a rose.

When I operated my consulting business, and during my tenure as an internal HR leader, I found that if I and my colleagues brought value to solving the people challenges within a business, without trying to take on the leadership accountabilities that appropriately belonged to others, we didn't have to ask for a seat at the table—we were dragged to it.

This approach for your HR function will reinforce the other elements of your "engine" to build high engagement, strong performance and capable leadership. It will create more capable leaders who can make good people-related decisions, understanding the solemn accountability they have in affecting others' lives and livelihoods.

WHAT ABOUT STARTUP COMPANIES?

Recognizing that some of you CEOs reading this book may be thinking, "These methods and principles are just too much for my company. We're still struggling to raise our next round of financing." Or you have not yet begun generating revenue, let alone profits.

It is true that the more rigorous principles and methods described here assume you have sufficient time and some resources to devote to them, such as the compensation methods that include market studies and variable compensation based on profitability, or the internal leadership development efforts that require dedicated time and capable program leaders.

Speaking from personal experience, I know how tenuous a new business can be, and how thin available time is to devote to anything other than survival. Every time I started a company, invested in a new business, or served on a board of a struggling organization, the existential nature of each day was the primary filter of determining priorities. Ironically, in such circumstances, the principles of engagement are needed the most, even as you may not feel you have the time to pay attention to them nor the resources to dedicate.

But the things you can do, even in challenging periods, are all the elements of engagement that have nothing to do with spending money or extra time. It's about *how you behave* while you're doing all the business tasks needed. You can lead people well, with care and candor, as a servant leader. You can be trustworthy and transparent about the business, your own objectives and why you made decisions. You can treat all people with respect. You can be inclusive, welcoming, and excited to have a wide variety of people join you. You can establish a meritocracy by how you evaluate contributions, how you make decisions about compensation and who is advanced to greater responsibility. You can form common values that are primary above all else. You can create a resonant purpose that speaks to the hearts of everyone in the business.

If you pay attention to these human factors during the tenuous early period of your business, or during a time of crisis, you are more likely to be successful both acutely and enduringly.

There is a dynamic in start-ups that can make applying what I'm suggesting very difficult, however. As a wizened entrepreneur once said to me early in my own business-building journey, "Be cautious about inviting others to invest in your business. You get a lot more than the money, and you may not like what you get."

Investors, by and large, are looking for a return on their cash. Well, it's not always *their* cash, of course. Many "strategic" investors and private equity firms use borrowed funds, especially if the borrowing costs are at a low point in the monetary cycle. Or they solicit investors who may be attracted to their investing strategy and then go looking for companies to buy or invest in. Most investors' expected horizon for achieving returns is typically a few short years, maybe three to five in total. Depending upon the terms of the investment, you may or may not have authority to direct the company's efforts and allocation of funds without approval of a board, or approval of investors who have negotiated decision rights over certain actions as a condition of providing their capital.

Even with such investors and dilution of your authority, things might go well for a while, without any impact to your ability to lead. You might be able to apply the range of leadership principles and methods described in this book, to good effect. But one day there may come a point where it all changes.

I've seen three things in companies aiming for an exit interfere with high-engagement principles in leading: when the company's existence is threatened, when the company is courting investors and when the company is nearing a lucrative "liquidity" event. Without redoubled leadership commitment all three conditions will potentially erode strong relationships. Add to the mix outside investors who have board representation and voting rights, and the fabric of cohesive engagement that you may have achieved to that point can begin to fray.

You might agree that when a business is at risk of failure, it's normal for relationships to be tested. But you might also wonder why potential good news, even great news, of a big pay day would cause fragmentation. Just like the Enron-Arthur Andersen example discussed earlier, the prospect of a huge financial gain can color how leaders (and investors) perceive the actions they may be taking. As one of my early mentors in the board room once said to me, "Sometimes money makes you stupid". Leadership behaviors that otherwise inspire people can be laid to the side, if by doing so the odds of that huge pay day are perceived to increase. Leaders may not even recognize when they are beginning to stray from their own values. They may even deny that they are.

In 1991, concurrent with the early growth of my consulting business, HRG Inc., I met a biochemist who had an idea for a novel DNA probe technology that would allow detecting multiple genetic targets in a single micro-well. At the time this would represent a big improvement in throughput and efficiency of conducting studies. It also could allow clinical diagnostic laboratories to greatly improve output and profitability. My co-founder suggested that we join because he didn't know anything about business. I certainly knew nothing about synthesizing artificial DNA. It seemed like good match. We formed a company, put some capital in and then began raising money.

When we first started, with little or nothing, we were very aligned. We wanted to do good work with authentic science and provide an enabling diagnostic platform for nucleic acid analyses. We wanted to be honest entrepreneurs.

We raised millions, opened a full lab, hired scientists and began making progress over the next several years. Or so I thought. The closer we got to performance milestones and as strategic partners started to show deeper interest in acquiring us, I began to detect a change in my co-founder's behavior. He started answering substantive questions obtusely. He would delay demonstrations for strategic partners. He would slow down discussions with one set of potential buyers and begin conversations with a new set, without coordinating with me or others. Board meetings became scavenger hunts to try to find the facts of the state of our technology, even as we were receiving letters of intent that would be significant in rewards to all our shareholders, especially him and me.

The person with whom I had started the company had changed before my eyes, or so it seemed. The truth, however, is that he was always the same person; I just didn't get to know him well enough before I joined him in the entrepreneurial boat. His values and ethics were situational, not enduring.

When I confronted him with his behavior and the evidence of subterfuge he reacted defensively and emotionally, not with facts. He couldn't accept that his great idea didn't pan out in practice. He kept kicking the can of proof down the road, hoping for a last-minute miracle to prove the technology, fudging results in the moment to be able to complete the sale of the company. The board and our potential suitors would not proceed without the proof, however.

The bits of our technology that were indeed proven were eventually sold off for enough to cover some of our liabilities, not all. Our investors received a goose egg. I got a capital loss to use against future gains, should I have any.

The point of this story is that if you are considering starting a business, who you partner with and who you invite as shareholders, is even more critical than the decision of who you hire. Your culture will be, always, the sum of the characters of the people involved. Make sure through long exploration and examination of the behavioral evidence that your values are aligned, before you jump in the boat.

As you proceed down the entrepreneurial path, you can test the engagement strength of the organization and its leadership. You can ask yourself, "Are we having more confidential, private meetings amongst leadership and the board? Are we sharing less about the company's condition with our people? Are we drafting organization charts and discussing individuals' futures based on various outcomes of decisions that we are considering, and we don't want people to know that this is going on? Are we hiding information from our board or our shareholders?" In other words, if transparency begins to blur, that's your first clue that you are leaving behind the principles of leadership that create engagement and results. And sound sleep for that matter.

One other issue to pay attention to is culture-washing. I have seen many new businesses born with great and lofty goals for the culture and the results, proudly espousing their long-term objectives of sustainable growth while elevating people to the highest priority. But the underlying purpose that really determined decisions was for the shareholders to find a quick and lucrative exit.

As I illustrated in my earlier example of the entrepreneurs who stated they wanted to create a highly engaged, enduring culture of stability while privately aiming to sell the company in three years, the contradictions will be evident to the people in the company, sooner or later. Again, hypocrisy is what kills culture fastest. There is nothing wrong with an entrepreneur or business owner stating that the goal is liquidity. Support and enthusiasm may well be the reaction, if she shares the rewards with the people who make it happen. That is congruent. People who join such a company are then aligned with the values and purpose. Not a problem.

What to do about these culture-eroding conditions is complex and you may not have the ability or right to direct the business in such cases. The best solution is to anticipate these dynamics during the period when you might be considering inviting outside investments or partners. If your fellow founders and investors are truly aligned with your leadership philosophy, your values and your purpose, there is less likelihood that these will be threatened over the course of their participation in your business.

The same is true for public companies. Garry literally spent decades finding and inviting the right long-term investors to be stockholders in WD-40 Company. Once they became owners of our stock, they stayed invested for many years. He would routinely ask them "What would make you want to sell your shares in our company?" The most heartening response we would hear was "If your engagement index begins to drop."

BUT THINGS HAVE CHANGED. HAVEN'T THEY?

The media are preoccupied as I write this with the advent of "generative artificial intelligence" (AI). All sorts of predictions are being offered by the observers of the trend, and great claims by companies looking for investment are presented, foretelling of step-function increases in scientific advances and productivity which are potentiated by AI.

Just as the internet (and the supporting technologies that caused it to be as pervasively useful as it is today) caused a metamorphosis in how many, many human activities are done, including economic relationships, there is no doubt that AI has the potential for yet another massive impact on how we all live and work. What will not change in the foreseeable future, in my opinion, is that most people on the planet will still need to provide some product or service in exchange for the means of living.

I could be wrong, of course. Maybe fusion energy will become a reality and provide limitless, clean energy at modest cost. With such an energy source, maybe all labor will be automated, from agriculture to building furniture to providing medical procedures to processing ore...everything. In such a world, a universal basic income could even be plausible.

Equally plausible in such a world would be the elimination of the need for any type of currency at all. Or self-sufficiency in any form. The automated, energized, self-organizing, self-evolving technologies we started will simply take over from there and put us out of the job of inventing or making anything ever again.

This future would mean organizations that gather people together for mutual economic benefit would have no reason to exist. And therefore, this nice book I just wrote would be absolutely useless.

The Economist published an article in its edition for week-ending June 2, 2023, entitled "Love and conflict", subtitle, "What would humans do in a world of ultra-powerful artificial intelligence?" The article references studies and published works by economists going back decades, related to the notion that expanding capabilities of technology might obviate the need for human production of goods or services.

It is true that the average annual hours worked per individual across most Western developed economies has declined over time, concurrent with the rise in technology-enabled productivity. According to the Economist article, in the U.S. in 1870 the average annual work year was over 3,000 hours, or about 60 hours a week. Just prior to the pandemic, it had dropped to an average of about 1,800 hours. Populations have risen dramatically in this same period, of course, and so has inflation-adjusted GDP.

Interestingly, as production of hard goods has become more automated, overall employment rates during the last century and a half have stayed relatively steady. Occasional contractions put a dent in employment, but recessions are shorter than periods of expansion. Services now make up about two-thirds of the economic activity in many developed economies. The history therefore shows that humans convert their type of work to that which technology cannot replicate, and which humans then place a premium on.

The Economist article cites the work of economist William Baumol in 1965 and more recent studies by economists Philippe Aghion, Ben Jones and Chad Jones in 2019, which align in showing that as technology takes over certain production and service capabilities from humans, the things that humans do which are more difficult to be automated rise in value and impact in the economy. Apparently, the very fact that a human produced something gives it a value premium, even if it is not as perfect as what a machine could produce.

Humans have evolved over millions of years, from the earliest primates to modern homo sapiens which first appeared about 300,000 years ago, and our psychology has been shaped by the environments that affected which traits and abilities would be passed on. Until just 10,000 years ago, humans didn't live in stationary settings. It was the advent of agriculture that allowed the first cities to appear. Our psychology is therefore built on hunter-gatherer society factors. But in the last century, and particularly since the middle of the twentieth century, technology has been changing faster than our generational rate of evolution. Even if we didn't have to lift a finger to stay alive, be comfortable and healthy, because AI would take care of us, we will still have the innate drive to create, to produce, to express, to push our boundaries, to engage with others, to have families, to sing, to dance, to paint, to write, to explore, to engage with life. These aspects of humanity are hard wired and can't change except slowly over millennia. Thus, they are valued. The exchange of what we value is the basis for any human economy.

I'm going to bet that people will continue to join together to create value and trade that value with others. That means organized effort, and therefore the principles of leadership to engage people, will remain relevant for many, many years to come.

CLOSING THOUGHTS

I was speaking recently with the CEO of a successful, growing e-commerce services company. The subject was organizational culture, and how to consciously create it. Coincidentally, another call a day later with the CFO of a 2,000-person biotech company on the East Coast was about the exact same thing.

It seems that the attention being paid to the concept of "culture" in a business has never been higher, since the point where it was famously introduced by the founder of modern management theory, Peter Drucker, in 2006 when he said, "Culture eats strategy for breakfast". Now, each day a new service firm is created to support what appears to be a growing market for guidance in building a desired culture.

It's always been a critical element of why some organizations endure and others don't. The form of the topic, its scope and perspective, its terminology have changed, however. Now, "culture" has come to be the most prominent word to describe the collection of behaviors that are considered required, or at least promoted, by those who hold the most authority and thus potential influence on the lives of others in the organization.

Long before Drucker uttered his now-famous phrase, there have been many approaches to deciding how an organization should collectively behave. Some are repugnant to our modern ear. There have been periods where organizational culture rested on concepts such as slavery, social class and even human interchangeability. This last phase started when scientific management practices were introduced by Frederick Taylor, an engineer, in the late 1800s. People were viewed as components in a human machine, with processes and procedures as the main topics, supported by data on the statistical range of human abilities, such as reaction time and visual acuity. Humans were, as in slavery, things to be placed on the game board of capitalism.

That view continued for quite a while, until the advent of collective bargaining and unionization of those interchangeable humans. Finally, the balance of control over economics shifted more evenly between the human "cogs" and the business owners. Then we automated away many of those unionized functions, and entered the era of the service economy, where non-product value exchanges form the largest segment of the economy. As the labor market tightens for knowledge workers and those in "essential" lines of service, unions aren't as necessary to equalize the bargaining power. Now organizations must appeal to the broader set of human motivations to maintain the economic viability of their companies. If most of your ability to generate revenue and profitability rests in the minds of people, who have increasing control to negotiate their remuneration (in the long run, as recessions do not last as long as economic growth cycles), you have to pay attention to the *quality* of their daily experience within the organization, in addition to compensation. Because that's what they want.

It's this last point that was the subject of my discussion with the biotech CFO. She understood that addressing the quality-of-life experience in her organization is fundamentally a business strategy for accomplishing any objective laid out ahead. Her leader, the COO, thinks it's only an issue of compensation, to find a way to compete with the reward structure of venture capital-backed biotech startups.

Psychologists have firmly established that after a certain income level, about the median for the U.S. for example, other factors start to become more important to a person than money. Like enjoying one's work, finding meaning in it, as part of a group that goes out of its way to help each other in good times and bad. Like seeing a path ahead for one's career and opportunities to learn, experience new things, applying one's aptitudes and interests for the benefit of all. Like feeling one's leader is admirable, trustworthy, and interested in one's well-being. Feeling safe in tough times.

So, a key reason "culture" is popular right now is that many business owners have realized they have to address the whole human, not the "cog" that scientific management describes. And eventually business owners and leaders realize that they, too, want work life to not suck. Why not enjoy the work, as a connected and committed team?

Another reason culture is topical is risk. Improving culture is viewed by some leaders as necessary to lower the chances of negative public relations, or to recover from scandal, and not an end in itself. The impact of social media has been huge in creating business risk resulting from what the public might think is inappropriate behavior within a company.

Here's the problem. No matter the organizational motivation, many leaders haven't yet realized or accepted the truth of what they say they want. That truth is: *creating a positive culture is about significant, authentic personal and collective behavior change.* A culture of high engagement is created through enduring, congruent, consistent daily behaviors that are intentionally chosen. These behaviors won't become unconscious and self-sustaining for a long time. It takes constant awareness, adjustment, and reinforcement. Depending upon how "far" the organization's current state is from the desired cultural description, it could take many years.

As CEO of the organization, you set the pace of personal change. And you can't stop paying attention to the daily actions needed because humans stray, hiring mistakes occur, promotional mistakes happen, leaders get tired of being the paragons of virtue all the time and values will always cost something to keep them, else they're not values.

It took me years to create a great culture at HRG, Inc. It took ongoing effort for decades at WD-40 Company. There are no short-cuts. But it can be seriously damaged in a matter of weeks or months. Depending upon the event, maybe even in minutes.

The first step in the wrong direction is taking the culture you've created, with high engagement and strong performance, for granted. If things are good for a long time, complacency is your first and worst enemy. You don't pick up on the cues that things are deteriorating. You fail to take action to protect the great culture you've built. You start to loosen the binding ropes of disciplined principles and behavioral practices. You assume it's all good and will stay good.

My philosophy of being a part of an organization is "I earn my right to be here every day." That is also my philosophy of leadership: "I earn the right to be a leader by how I behave every day." Each day, every day, for as long as I serve in the role. That's what it takes to create and maintain the type of human cohesion and commitment which are such powerful determinants of not only how the organization performs, but also what the quality of life is like to be part of it.

If it's not obvious to you yet, this book is simply about *how* you lead. It is through conscious leadership, intent upon achieving the organizational culture that you aspire to, that you succeed.

It's not a matter of cost. There's no "app" for it. It doesn't take much more time than you're already devoting. It's about investing your *attention*, to practice the principles which cause people to say they love to work for your organization, they are optimistic about their own future and the future of the company, they feel that their immediate leader is both a coach and a mentor, they feel like they belong.

It's about constructing your business model and cost structure in a way that protects people from the risk of losing their jobs because you can't afford them anymore, so they feel safe enough to quit looking for other opportunities and truly think long term about their contributions.

It's about treating people like accountable adults, not "taking care" of them like a parent.

It's about being a meritocracy where anyone, from any background or category of human, can earn their advancement by demonstrating their abilities to contribute. It's about aligning pay and opportunities with those demonstrated competencies and contributions, in a market-driven approach to compensation.

It's about having values which are lived daily and incorporated into everything you do.

It's about being open and transparent with people about every aspect of the business and how it affects them personally, within regulatory and legal constraints. Especially about how decisions of hiring, promotion, compensation and job assignments are made.

The rewards for the discipline you apply as a leader will be massive. I'm talking about the feeling, the quality of experience that you can achieve when your company operates as a tight team who likes working together, sharing the hard work and the celebrations with excitement. You'll create a culture where people have each other's backs, where people excel as individuals and succeed together.

If you aren't where you want to be yet, relax. There are no short cuts, no formula or recipe that will get you to your organizational goal in a few short weeks or months. But that's okay. The joy is in every step along the adventure, not at the finish line. Because there isn't one.

My hope is that you have found some value in this book, to help you on your personal cultural journey as CEO.

ABOUT THE AUTHOR

Stan Sewitch is a business psychologist, entrepreneur and lifelong student of human behavior in the world of work. He has founded four companies: HRG Inc. (organizational consulting), Emlyn Systems (HRIS software), Chromagen (biotech diagnostics) and KI Investment Holdings (private equity). Since retiring from WD-40 Company, Stan continues working with business leaders and owners on strategy, organizational design, culture, leadership development and related topics, through Sewitch Etcetera Corporation: https://www.stansewitch.com

Stan holds an M.S. in Industrial Psychology from California State University at Long Beach, and a B.A. in Psychology from San Diego State University. Both degrees emphasized the neurological bases of behavior.

Stan was a weekly columnist for the San Diego Daily Transcript for ten years, writing "Notes from the Corporate Underground", illuminating the sometimes-hidden world of human thought and feelings within organizations. Stan published two volumes of selections from his column: "Paradise is not for Sissies" and "Work for a Jerk and Love It".

He has held multiple senior leadership positions across a variety of functions, including sales, manufacturing, quality assurance, human resources and multiple CEO roles. He has served as a director for 13 private companies since 1989, ranging from start-ups to over $200 million in annual sales.

As an advisor and then as global HR leader for WD-40 Company, Stan partnered with former CEO Garry Ridge and senior leaders for over 20 years to build the engine of a highly engaged, high performing organization.